Rabbi Jonathan Cahn is a Jewish prophet who has been chosen to reveal end-time mysteries—vital material to put the last-days puzzle together!

—SID ROTH
HOST, *IT'S SUPERNATURAL!*

The Mystery of the Shemitah is a detailed, compelling, and provocative book for anyone seeking answers to the future of America and the world.

—MARCUS D. LAMB
FOUNDER, PRESIDENT, DAYSTAR TELEVISION NETWORK

The Mystery of the Shemitah is the most amazing thing I have ever read! Brilliant and stunning…sobering…humbling…it is undeniable truth. It is one of the most important books of our lifetime!

—JOSEPH FARAH
FOUNDER, WND

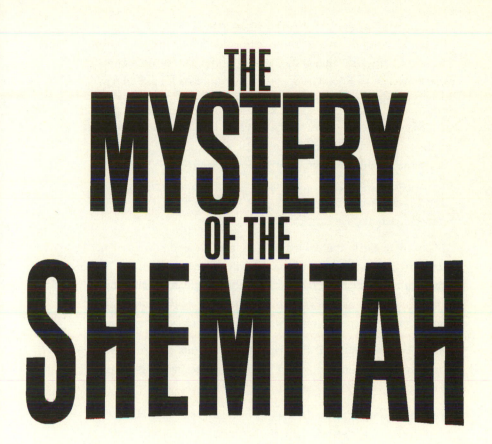

THE
MYSTERY
OF THE
SHEMITAH

JONATHAN CAHN

Most CHARISMA HOUSE BOOK GROUP products are available at special quantity discounts for bulk purchase for sales promotions, premiums, fund-raising, and educational needs. For details, write Charisma House Book Group, 600 Rinehart Road, Lake Mary, Florida 32746, or telephone (407) 333-0600.

THE MYSTERY OF THE SHEMITAH WITH DVD by Jonathan Cahn
Published by FrontLine
Charisma Media/Charisma House Book Group
600 Rinehart Road
Lake Mary, Florida 32746
www.charismahouse.com

Cover design by Justin Evans

Library of Congress Control Number: 2015945095
International Standard Book Number: 978-1-62998-715-6

First edition

15 16 17 18 19 — 987654321
Printed in the United States of America

CONTENTS

PART I

ORIGINS OF THE MYSTERY

Chapter 1

A MYSTERY of
THREE THOUSAND YEARS

Is It Possible...?

Is it possible that there exists a three-thousand-year-old mystery that lies behind everything from the implosion of the New York Stock Exchange, the collapse of the American and world economy, the attack of 9/11, the rise of nations, the fall of nations, and events that have not yet happened but are yet to take place?

- Is it possible that the words of an ancient text are determining and controlling the future of the financial realm, the business realm, and the economic realm?

- Is it possible that an ordinance given to a relatively small and obscure Middle Eastern nation is now determining the future of every nation on earth?

- Is it possible that a spiritual principle given to a nation of shepherds and farmers lies behind the expansion and collapse of virtually every stock market in the world?

- Is it possible that a mystery begun over three thousand years ago on a desert mountain pinpoints the exact time, down to dates and hours, of some of the most critical events of modern times?

- And is it possible that this mystery is even now governing the future of everyone reading these words and the lives of most inhabitants of this planet?

It may sound like something one would expect to find in a Hollywood fantasy or science fiction—but it's real—as real as any phenomenon could be.

Much that will be revealed in this book has never before been revealed in written form. Most people have never heard of the word *shemitah*, much less the mystery that surrounds it. Yet their lives have been critically impacted, altered, or determined by its manifestation.

It all begins on a desert mountaintop upon which a bearded time-worn man stands waiting for a revelation. The revelation will come. And after the old man descends the mountain, it will continue through a series of supernatural encounters in the desert wilderness. It is within this revelation that the mystery of the Shemitah will begin.

The revelation will continue to unfold as a weeping prophet walks the ground on which had once stood the holy city, the glory of his nation. Now it lies in ruins and rubble. The reason for its destruction, the timing of the calamity, and the nature of its judgment are all contained in the Shemitah and the mystery surrounding it.

The mystery will continue to unfold beyond ancient times, through centuries and ages, until reaching the modern world.

It will embrace America's rise to world power, the collapse of Wall Street and stock markets around the world, the march of Allied soldiers across Europe and into Berlin, the postwar global order, the events of 9/11, the Great Recession, and much more.

The mystery will converge with a second dynamic, the mystery of the towers, a phenomenon that begins with the construction of Babel and extends to the ruins of Ground Zero.

The mystery of the Shemitah will not only operate on a massive and global stage but also on the smallest of scales, altering bank accounts, determining the financial well-being or the lack of it for those who have fathomed that such a phenomenon exists, changing the course of their lives.

In recent years economic and financial analysts have been at a loss for words as they watched the collapse of the world's economic and financial realms. And yet we will find that the secret behind these phenomena lies not with the opinions of modern pundits but in words of ancient parchments.

The mystery was first revealed in *The Harbinger: The Ancient Mystery That Holds the Secret of America's Future.* I take no credit for the book or the revelations therein. I wasn't looking to write a book, nor was I seeking to come up with any message or revelation. It began without being sought after and then basically wrote itself. *The Harbinger* contains fourteen major revelations or mysteries. One of these revelations is that of the Shemitah.

From the moment the book was released, I've been deluged with questions concerning America's future and that of the world. In particular, *The Harbinger*'s seventeenth chapter, which reveals the link between the ancient Shemitah and the events of modern times, has prompted a whirlwind of speculation. With the approach of the next Shemitah, the amount of speculation has increased exponentially. In view of this, FrontLine, publisher of *The Harbinger*, strongly felt that a book had to be written to open up the mystery of the Shemitah. They approached me with the idea.

My initial reaction was caution because I didn't want the message or warning contained in *The Harbinger* to get lost in date-setting. *The Harbinger*'s ultimate call is that of repentance, not speculation or the setting of dates. The mysteries contained in *The Harbinger* all point to a coming national calamity concerning America and the world. But that calamity doesn't have to take place when we think it must or according to schedule. The judgment and calamity revealed and warned about in *The Harbinger* do not depend on any set date or time parameter. But barring a national change of course, it will come. The most important thing, no matter when it comes, is to be ready and to be right with God.

There was much more to the mystery of the Shemitah than what I was able to reveal in *The Harbinger*'s one chapter concerning it—so much more that it would take an entire book to reveal it. That is the reason for this book. What could not be revealed before will be revealed now. In fact, as it was with

The Harbinger, most of the mysteries to be revealed in the following pages have never up to this point been revealed.

We now embark on an expedition to find the pieces of an ancient mystery. We will then begin placing the pieces together until the mystery is revealed. In the process we will answer these questions:

- Could there be an ancient phenomenon lying beneath some of the most critical events of modern times?

- Could this phenomenon be operating behind some of the most dramatic and monumental collapses of Wall Street and the global economy?

- Could this phenomenon underlie some of the most colossal events of modern times?

- Could this phenomenon from ancient times be so precise that it has not only determined events in the modern world but also ordained their timing, down to exact dates, hours, even minutes?

- Could this phenomenon already be affecting, shaping, and altering our lives and the lives of virtually everyone we know?

- Does this ancient mystery hold the key to what the future holds, what is yet to come?

- Are there signs and harbingers warning us of what lies ahead?

- Will the American age as we know it continue for many more years, or will we witness its end?

- Is America in danger of a coming calamity, a collapse, even judgment?

- What does the future hold for the world?

Let us now begin the search.

Chapter 2

The ISAIAH KEY

The Warnings

COULD GOD SEND a warning as He did to people and nations in ancient times, but now to people and nations of the modern world?

The Bible reveals a clear pattern: before judgment, God warns. In the days of ancient Israel God sent warning of impending national judgment through varied means, through visions, through dreams, through audible voices, through prophetic utterances, through signs, through the written word, through prophetic acts, through supernatural occurrences, and through the outworking of natural events.

The Bible states that God does not change. He is the same yesterday, today, and forever. We must therefore conclude that not only *can* God send a prophetic warning into the modern world but also, where judgment is concerned, He *will* send warning. So in the case of a nation standing in danger of impending calamity or destruction, we can expect that such warning will be given, and in a way consistent with those given in biblical times.

The Day of the Towers

The Harbinger is a book that reveals an ancient biblical mystery manifesting in modern times. It is a message of warning concerning coming calamity. How and when did it come forth?

It began on the morning of September 11, 2001. Ten years earlier I had been led to give a message in which I spoke of a national judgment beginning in New York City. I shared that message not far from the city, as the two ministries I lead, Hope of the World and the Jerusalem Center/Beth Israel, are both located in northern New Jersey, across the river from Manhattan.

On the evening of September 11 I was staring across the Hudson River at the massive cloud of smoke that covered the ground of destruction and much of lower Manhattan. Later on, in prayer concerning the national calamity, I was led to turn to the ninth and tenth chapters of the Book of Isaiah.

These chapters contained the verse from which the revelations of *The Harbinger* would come. At the time I didn't zero in on that specific verse. I was more focused on the overall context, which was that of a nation undergoing the first warning

stroke of national judgment, a warning in the form of a strike
of terror on the land.

The Isaiah Key

The event that proved to be the turning point would take place
sometime later at the corner of Ground Zero. I was standing
on a plot of soil near where the towers had fallen. My attention
became transfixed on an object. The object was a tree that had
been struck down by the force of the calamity. I heard an inner
voice say, "There's a mystery here. You must seek and find it."
So I began to search into the mystery that had so drawn my
attention.

I was immediately led to the same section of Isaiah to which
I opened in the wake of 9/11. But this time my attention was
drawn to one specific verse in Isaiah's prophecy, the verse that
would open the door to the revelations that would be known as
The Harbinger. The revelation concerned nine prophetic signs
of warning and judgment. The fallen tree was the first puzzle
piece of an ancient mystery that kept growing bigger and bigger.

The Puzzle Pieces

One by one, each of the nine signs were revealed. Whenever the
mystery seemed to come to a standstill, the next leading would
be given. It would come in the form of someone saying a word
that proved to be the next key in the puzzle. At other times it
would come by an inner sense, which, upon investigation, would
prove true. Still, at other times it would come in the form of
"accidents"—something appearing out of the blue on my computer screen that contained the key I had been searching for, or,
at other times, what I had *not* been searching for.

The Genesis of *The Harbinger*

I first shared the revelations of *The Harbinger* at a Friday night service of my congregation. The people who heard it were stunned. There was an immediate feeling that it was a message that had to go forth to the nation. But I didn't take any action in that direction until two years later when I was led to commit the revelations to writing.

In 2005, while sharing the initial revelations, I alluded to a coming collapse of Wall Street. In September 2008, in the midst of writing the book, Wall Street did collapse. The collapse triggered the Great Recession. It would also trigger the opening of a new stream of ancient mysteries and revelations. It was in this stream that the mystery of the Shemitah began to unfold.

In the process of writing *The Harbinger*, I was led to present the mysteries and revelations in a way that would be easy for anyone to grasp. The Bible uses parables, allegories, stories, symbols, and imagery to communicate spiritual and prophetic truth. I was led to do likewise. So *The Harbinger* presents a story that serves as a vessel through which the mysteries and revelations unfold.

The Prophet and the Nine Seals

The narrative involves a mysterious figure simply known as "the prophet," and another named Nouriel, a writer and journalist. Nouriel receives a mysterious gift. It appears to be an ancient clay seal. Across the face of the seal is an inscription in a foreign script. The seal remains a mystery to Nouriel until its meaning is revealed to him by the prophet.

Their first encounter takes place in what appears to be a chance meeting on a park bench overlooking the Hudson River. In the course of their subsequent encounters the prophet gives Nouriel nine clay seals. Each of the seals contains a mystery that Nouriel must seek to unlock. Each mystery is connected to a harbinger of warning and judgment now manifesting on American soil.

The entire story came to me in a matter of hours. As soon as I began committing it to writing, with the voice of the prophet bringing forth each of the revelations, the words came out in rapid-fire succession. With no struggle and little effort the text flowed onto the pages. *The Harbinger* seemed to write itself. And in a relatively short time it was finished.

The Going Forth

From that moment onward the message of *The Harbinger* has taken on a life of its own. From the story of how it became a book to the way it went forth to the nation, it has proceeded apart from anyone's planning and has involved several uncanny events in defiance of any natural explanation. It has now been read, seen, or heard by millions and has reached the highest echelons of government—to the point of being spoken of on Capitol Hill by members of Congress and presidential candidates. From the moment of its inception until now, it has borne the marks of another's fingerprints.

In order to open up the mystery of the Shemitah, we must first open up, even briefly, the mystery from which it comes—that of the mystery of *The Harbinger*. What exactly is the mystery of *The Harbinger*? What are the nine harbingers that have manifested in our lifetime? And what secret do they hold concerning our future?

To this we now turn.

Chapter 3

The MYSTERY of the
NINE HARBINGERS

The Harbinger

T*HE HARBINGER* IS the revealing of an ancient mystery that
holds the secret of what has happened and is happening to
America and the world in modern times—a mystery that lies
behind everything from 9/11 to the collapse of Wall Street and
the global economy—a mystery spanning thousands of years,
in which an ancient text ordains the words uttered by world

12

leaders, who have no idea w\
times and dates given more t\
the time and dates on which\
events of recent times take pl\

The mysteries contained w\
financial realm, the economic\
cultural realm, and the lives, co\
now reading these words.

The mystery begins in the la_____, the
northern kingdom, as nine harbi_____ ʌ.ophetic signs, warnings of national judgment and destruction, appear in the land.
The nation is given a period of grace to either change its course
or head to destruction. However, the people and their leaders
respond not with repentance but with defiance. They continue
on their course of moral and spiritual apostasy. In a matter of
years the nation will be wiped off the face of the earth.

What is eerie, stunning, scary, or amazing is that these
same nine harbingers of judgment are now reappearing in
modern times—on American soil. Some appeared in New
York City. Others have appeared in Washington DC. Some
have manifested in the form of objects; others, as events. Some
have involved ceremonies. Still others have involved American
leaders, even the president of the United States. They have
happened with specificity, precision, consistency, and without
anyone's conscious intent or action to make them happen. The
same harbingers that once warned an ancient nation of judgment now warn America and the world of the same thing.

THE NINE HARBINGERS OF JUDGMENT

What are the nine harbingers of judgment that appeared in
ancient Israel years before the destruction of that kingdom?

(page corner folded, partially showing: "14" · "In the space we hav... mysteries conta... touch upon ...")

e here, we can't even begin to explore the
ned in *The Harbinger*—but we can briefly
hem.

THE FIRST HARBINGER: THE BREACH

Sign of the Breach: Years before the judgment of a nation
there comes a warning, a national shaking. The warning manifests in the form of an attack. The nation's hedge of protection,
its natural security, is breached. The attack is temporary and
contained, but it will constitute the nation's wake-up call, the
"opening bell" of judgment concerning the nation's future.

Ancient Appearance: It manifested in ancient Israel in
732 BC, when the nation's hedge of protection was breached
through an enemy attack. The attack was temporary and contained, a wake-up call for a people who had grown so deafened
to God's voice that nothing else would get through.

The Reappearance: It manifested in America on September
11, 2001, as the nation's hedge of protection was breached
through an enemy attack. The attack was temporary and contained, a wake-up call for a people who had grown so deafened to God's voice that nothing else would get through—the
first of the nine harbingers of judgment. In the wake of 9/11,
America would begin eerily reenacting the actions of ancient
Israel in its last days as a nation. The same objects, actions,
events, and words would manifest, one after the other, just as
they did in the days before Israel's judgment.

THE SECOND HARBINGER: THE TERRORIST

Sign of the Terrorist: The opening strike of judgment, the
breach of the nation's hedge of protection, is not only a military action but also an act of terrorism. It is masterminded

and carried out by those who employ terror as a means to accomplish their ends.

Ancient Appearance: This harbinger manifested in ancient Israel as those who masterminded the attack were the Assyrians—the world's first terrorists and the fathers of all terrorists, employing terror as a strategic means to accomplish a political goal.

The Reappearance: It manifested on American soil as the attack was masterminded by the modern counterparts of the ancient Assyrians, their spiritual children, who even carried out the attack using the sister language to that spoken by those who attacked ancient Israel. September 11 would even cause American soldiers to fight on the soil of ancient Assyria.

THE VOW OF DEFIANCE

After the attack in 732 BC the people of Israel made a vow. The words of that vow were recorded by the prophet Isaiah: "The bricks have fallen, but we will rebuild with hewn stone; the sycamores have been cut down, but we will plant cedars in their place."[1]

The vow was an act of defiance. The nation was saying: "You will not humble us. We will not repent. We will not turn back. Rather, we will continue to depart from Your ways. We will rebuild. We will replant. And by our own power and resources, we will come back stronger than before—against You."

So in place of repentance was pride, and in place of humility, arrogance. And the vow would become the key to the nine harbingers. It would set the course for national destruction.

THE THIRD HARBINGER: THE FALLEN BRICKS

"The bricks have fallen…"

Sign of the Fallen Bricks: The first act of warning and judgment is marked by the image of falling, collapsing buildings. This, and the ruin heaps that will stand in their place, become the most tangible sign and the most concrete image of the calamity.

Ancient Appearance: The most tangible signs of what took place in 732 BC were the ruin heaps of the buildings that the Assyrians had destroyed.

The Reappearance: The most tangible sign of 9/11 was that of the falling towers and the ruin heaps that stood in their place.

THE FOURTH HARBINGER: THE TOWER

"But we will rebuild…"

Sign of the Tower: The nation under judgment returns to the ground of destruction and vows to rebuild the fallen buildings, but now bigger, taller, and stronger than before. The reconstruction becomes a symbol of the nation's attempt at a defiant resurgence. According to the most ancient translation of Scripture, it will take the form of a rising tower.

Ancient Appearance: In the wake of the Assyrian attack the people of Israel vowed to rebuild the fallen buildings and build them bigger, better, and stronger than before. Rising up from the ruin heaps would be walls, dwellings, and towers.

The Reappearance: In the wake of 9/11 America embarked on a campaign to rebuild the ruins. From the ground of destruction a tower began to rise. The resulting edifice would be the greatest object of defiance ever erected on American soil.

THE FIFTH HARBINGER: THE GAZIT STONE

"...we will rebuild with hewn stone..."

, **Sign of the Gazit Stone:** After the attack the people carve out a massive rectangular block of stone from mountain rock. They then bring it to the site of destruction, where the bricks had fallen, and there set it down in place. The stone will be the first embodiment of their vow of defiance.

Ancient Appearance: The people of Israel vowed to rebuild, not with the clay bricks that had fallen, but with "hewn stone," the Hebrew *gazit*, indicating a massive rectangular block of stone chiseled out of mountain rock. They go up to the mountains and bedrock of the land, carve out the massive stones, and bring them back to the ground of destruction where they vow to rebuild and come back stronger than before.

The Reappearance: On July 4, 2004, the fifth harbinger reappeared on American soil. It was a gazit stone, chiseled out of the mountains of New York, brought back to New York City, and lowered onto the floor of Ground Zero. A ceremony took place around it, during which American leaders pronounced vows of national defiance.

THE SIXTH HARBINGER: THE SYCAMORE

"The sycamores have been cut down..."

Sign of the Sycamore: The attack not only causes the fall of buildings but also the striking down of trees—one particular kind of tree—the sycamore, a sign of national judgment.

Ancient Appearance: It manifested in ancient Israel as the sycamores were struck down in the midst of the attack.

The Reappearance: On September 11 the sixth harbinger manifested on American soil as the falling tower struck down a tree—a sycamore, the ancient sign of national judgment—at the corner of Ground Zero.

THE SEVENTH HARBINGER: THE EREZ TREE

"But we will plant cedars in their place."

Sign of the Erez Tree: In the wake of the calamity the people resolve to plant another tree in the same exact soil in which the sycamore had been struck down. The second tree is not a sycamore but a stronger one. The English *cedar* stands for the Hebrew *erez* tree—a conifer, an evergreen, a pinacea tree—a tree to symbolize their self-confident hope in their resurgence.

Ancient Appearance: The people of Israel planted erez trees in the place of the fallen sycamores, another sign of their defiance and their resolve to come back stronger than before.

The Reappearance: Two years after the calamity the seventh harbinger manifested in America. It appeared at the corner of Ground Zero in the form of a tree. The tree replaced the fallen sycamore. It stood in the very same soil. It was not a sycamore. It was a Hebrew erez tree, just as in ancient Israel. People gathered around it in a ceremony and gave it its name: the Tree of Hope.

THE EIGHTH HARBINGER: THE UTTERANCE

Sign of the Utterance: A national leader utters the vow of Isaiah 9:10. The vow is spoken as a public declaration, the sign of a nation in defiance of God. By uttering the vow, the leader pronounces judgment on the land.

Ancient Appearance: The vow was uttered by one or more of Israel's leaders, as only a leader can speak for a nation and determine its course. The vow, intended as a rallying cry, instead pronounced judgment and set the stage for destruction.

The Reappearance: On the third anniversary of 9/11 a famous American leader spoke before a congressional caucus, and out of his mouth proceeded the ancient vow of defiance. He unwittingly pronounced judgment on America. He even built his entire speech around the ancient vow of destruction.

THE NINTH HARBINGER: THE PROPHECY

Sign of the Prophecy: A national leader utters the vow soon after the calamity, speaking prophetically, proclaiming that which would take place, becoming part of the national record, and setting the nation's course to judgment.

Ancient Appearance: Soon after the attack of 732 BC a leader uttered the vow, speaking of what would take place before it did, being recorded by the prophet Isaiah, and setting the nation's course to judgment.

The Reappearance: On September 12, 2001, the day after the calamity, the American Congress gathered on Capitol Hill to issue the nation's response. The man appointed to speak for the nation was the Senate majority leader. There before the United States Senate and House of Representatives, the nation, and the world, he proclaimed the ancient vow of defiance, setting the nation's course to judgment.[2] He had no idea what he was saying, but he identified America as a nation in defiance of God and under judgment. His words would come true. He spoke of the harbingers, the tree that was struck down, the stone that would go up, and the replacing of the one tree with the other. He set the course of defiance and set the stage for the second shaking of the nation.

The Second Shaking

The nine harbingers are not the end of the story but the beginning. The mysteries continue. *The Harbinger* reveals the biblical progression of national judgment. If a nation does not heed the warning of the first shaking, there comes a second.

The second shaking of America did not involve the destruction of buildings. Rather, it involved the shaking of American power itself. As with 9/11, it not only affected America but also the world. The second shaking involved the collapse of American financial and economic power, beginning with the implosion of Wall Street.

Behind this shaking is a stream of biblical mysteries, one of which gives the exact time and the exact dates, down to the hours. We have time here to just briefly mention them.

The Isaiah 9:10 Effect

An ancient biblical principle from the last days of Israel reveals how America's response to the first shaking, specific actions taken in the days immediately following 9/11, would bring about, years later, the collapse of the American and global economies.

The Buttonwood Mystery

On the day America began its rise to global financial superpower, a sign appeared. On September 11, 2001, the same sign reappeared but in a different form—foreshadowing not the rise of a greater power, but warning of its coming fall.

The Mystery of the Third Witness

Scripture ordains that before a matter of judgment is executed, there must be two or three witnesses, two or three who bear consistent testimony concerning the matter. *The Harbinger* reveals that in the case of America and judgment, all three witnesses have appeared. The third witness is the president of the United States.

The Harbinger Continues:
The New Manifestations

Since *The Harbinger* came out, the harbingers and mysteries revealed in the book are continuing to manifest. What is spoken of in the book is coming true. The mystery of judgment has continued to progress.

- One of these concerns the seventh harbinger and a clear biblical sign foretelling the judgment of nations.

- Another concerns a prophetic word hidden in the ruins of Ground Zero.

- Another concerns the fourth harbinger, the tower, the president of the United States, and eight words that lead to national destruction.

- Another concerns a message sent out to millions in America and around the world, confirming the link of Isaiah 9:10 to September 11, 2001, but given years before the calamity took place.

- Another concerns an event that took place long before America became a nation and connected to the giving of the message of *The Harbinger* itself.

The continuation of the signs is itself a sign that America has continued its descent from God. As the apostasy progresses, so do the harbingers of judgment.

The Mystery Ground

One other mystery revealed in *The Harbinger* warranting mention here is that of the mystery ground. Embedded in America's foundation is a prophetic warning. The warning was given on America's first day as a nation. It concerns what will happen if America should ever turn away from God. Linked to that same day and that warning is a ground of earth—America's ground of consecration. It is here the nation was dedicated to God at its birth. It is this ground which joins together ancient Israel, 9/11, and a prophetic warning to America for this hour.

The Mystery of the Shemitah

There is yet another mystery in *The Harbinger* we haven't mentioned—for the reason that we will now devote the rest of this book to revealing it. Having now set the prophetic context, we will now begin to unlock that ancient mystery that has not only determined the course of modern history and modern events in America and the nations, but has also ordained the very timing of those events, down to the days—even down to the hours—the mystery of the Shemitah.

In order to unlock it, we must find and assemble five keys...

PART II

THE MYSTERY OF THE SHEMITAH AND THE FIVE KEYS

Chapter 4

FIRST KEY:
The SEVENTH YEAR

The Man on the Mountain

THE MYSTERY BEGINS in a Middle Eastern desert. An aged
man ascends a mountain. The mountain is shaking and
appears to be on fire, with flashes of lightning and thunderous
rumblings of what sounds like a blasting trumpet. Gathered around the mountain's base are multiplied thousands of
people, watching in fear.

25

The old man reaches the mountain's peak and enters into the midst of a thick cloud. Within the cloud he is given a revelation. The man is called "Moshe" and will be known to much of the world as Moses. From the revelation given him will come the commandments, the moral laws, the dietary laws, the laws of cleansings, the blueprint of the tent known as the *mishkan* or "tabernacle," the establishment of priesthood and the sacrifices, the laws of the Sabbath and holy days, and all the details that will make up the foundation upon which the nation of Israel will rest. The revelation will be called the *Torah* or the "Law." It is from this revelation that the mystery of the Shemitah will arise.

The Sabbath of Years

It is well known that, for the nation of Israel, every seventh day was called "the Sabbath." The Sabbath was unique among days. The Israelites were commanded to keep it separate and distinct from the other six days of the week. It was holy. It was the Lord's Day. On the Sabbath all regular work and all worldly endeavors were to cease. The Sabbath was the day of rest, to be devoted solely to the Lord.

But what is not well known is that the Sabbath was not only a day but also a year. As every seventh day was the Sabbath day, so every seventh year was the Sabbath year.

> The LORD spoke to Moses on Mount Sinai, saying, "Speak to the children of Israel and say to them: 'When you come to the land which I give you, then the land shall keep a Sabbath to the LORD. Six years shall you sow your field, and six years you shall prune your vineyard, and gather its fruits; but in the seventh year there shall be a sabbath of solemn rest for the land, a sabbath to the LORD.'"
> —LEVITICUS 25:1–4

The Sabbath year was likewise to be kept separate and distinct from the six years that preceded it. It was to be a holy year, a year specially devoted to the Lord. During the Sabbath year there was to be no working of the land. All sowing and reaping, all plowing and planting, all gathering and harvesting had to cease by the end of the sixth year.

> Six years you shall sow your land and gather in its produce,
> but the seventh year you shall let it rest and lie fallow...
> —EXODUS 23:10–11

During the Sabbath year it was not only for the people to rest, but also the land. The fields would lie fallow, the vineyards untended, and the groves unkept. The land itself would observe its own Sabbath to the Lord.

> ...that the poor of your people may eat; and what they leave, the beasts of the field may eat. In like manner you shall do with your vineyard and your olive grove.
> —EXODUS 23:11

During the Sabbath year the people of Israel were to leave their fields, vineyards, and groves open for the poor. For the duration of the year the land belonged, in effect, to everyone. And whatever grew of its own accord was called *hefker*, meaning, "without an owner." So during the Sabbath year the land, in effect, belonged to everyone and no one at the same time.

Elul 29

Just as striking as what happened to the land during the Sabbath year was what happened to the people on the last day of that year:

> At the end of every seven years you shall grant a release
> of debts. And this is the form of the release: Every cred-
> itor who has lent anything to his neighbor shall release
> it; he shall not require it of his neighbor or his brother,
> because it is called the LORD's release.
>
>   —DEUTERONOMY 15:1–2

"At the end of every seven years" refers to the last day of the Sabbath year. Elul was the last month of the Hebrew civil year, and the twenty-ninth day was the last day of Elul. So on Elul 29, the very last day of the Sabbath year, a sweeping transformation took place in the nation's financial realm. Everyone who owed a debt was released. And every creditor had to release the debt owed. So on Elul 29 all credit was erased and all debt was wiped away. The nation's financial accounts were, in effect, wiped clean. It was Israel's day of financial nullification and remission.

In the Hebrew reckoning of time, each day begins not with the morning but with the night. This goes back to Genesis 1, when the account of Creation records that there was first darkness, night, and then the day. So every Hebrew day begins with the night before the day. And since night begins with sunset, every Hebrew day begins at sunset. Therefore the moment that all debts had to be reckoned as wiped away was the sunset of Elul 29.

The Remission

In English, the Elul 29 command ordains that every creditor shall "grant a release." But the original Hebrew commands every creditor to make a "shemitah." In those first two verses of Deuteronomy 15 the word *shemitah* appears no less than four times. At the end of the second verse it is written, "Because it is called the Lord's release." In Hebrew it is called the Lord's "Shemitah."

The word *shemitah* is most often translated as "the release" or "the remission." The English word *remission* is defined as "the cancellation or reduction of a debt or penalty." The Shemitah of ancient Israel refers not only to the releasing of the land but also to the nullification of debt and credit ordained by God and performed on a massive nationwide scale.

Shemitah became the name of the last day of the Sabbath year, Elul 29, the Day of Remission. But it also became the name of the Sabbath year in its entirety. The seventh year would become known as the Year of the Shemitah, or simply, the Shemitah. The Year of the Shemitah would begin with the releasing of the land and end with the Day of Remission, when the people would themselves be released.

So the word *shemitah* covers both the seventh year and the last day of that year. There's a reason for that. That last day of Elul 29 is the year's crescendo, its peak and culmination—the remission of the Year of Remission. In a sense, everything about the Shemitah year builds up to that final day, when everything is released, remitted, and wiped away in one day—or, more specifically, to the eve of that day, to the final sunset.

The Radical Ramifications

The idea of a nation ceasing all work on its land for an entire year is a radical proposition. No less radical is the idea of a day in which all credit and debt are wiped away. The ramifications of these two requirements are so great that concerns arose in later generations as to the Shemitah's financial and economic consequences. These concerns were intensified when the Jewish people returned to the land of Israel in modern times.

In order to resolve these concerns, the rabbis sought to come up with ways of avoiding the Shemitah's more radical requirements. One of these was based on the idea that the Shemitah applied primarily to Jewish-owned land. So in the Year of the Shemitah, Jewish farmers would sell their lands to non-Jews and continue to work. The selling would be done under an agreement in which the land would revert to the Jewish farmer at the end of the Shemitah year.

In the same way, the rabbis devised ways to get around the cancellation of debts. The rabbinical sage Hillel developed a system whereby debts could be transferred to a religious court. Since a court is not an individual, the debt would survive the Year of the Shemitah. Still others came up with other strategies around it. So the Shemitah continued to be observed, in one form or another, but those forms became increasingly symbolic.

Not everyone accepted these methods. Orthodox Jews in Israel tell stories of Jewish farmers who faithfully kept the Shemitah's requirement without any alteration and ended up with an extra abundant harvest the following year. Regardless of the controversy surrounding them, the fact that these methods were devised by the rabbis reveals two things that will prove important in unlocking the mystery of the Shemitah:

1. The Shemitah bears consequences that specifically affect the financial and economic realm.

2. The effects of the Shemitah bear key similarities to the effects of an economic and financial collapse.

The Call of the Shemitah

What was the reason for the Shemitah in the first place? There are several answers—all of which touch the spiritual realm.

The Shemitah bears witness that the land and, for that matter, the earth, belong to God. It is only entrusted to man as a steward. God is sovereign. His sovereignty extends also to the realms of money, finances, economies, and possessions. These are entrusted to man's keeping but ultimately belong to God.

The Shemitah declares that God is first and above all realms of life, and must therefore be put first and above every realm. During the Shemitah Israel was, in effect, compelled to turn away from these earthly or worldly realms and turn to the spiritual.

The Shemitah cleanses and wipes away, ends imbalances, levels accounts, and nullifies that which has built up in the previous years—a massive cleansing of the financial and economic slate. It ends entanglements and brings release. Its release applies not only to the land and to the nation's financial accounts, but also to something much more universal. The Shemitah requires the people to release their attachments to the material realm: their possessions, their finances, their real estate, and their claims and pursuits concerning such things. It is the breaking of bonds. And those who release are, likewise, released, no longer possessed by their possessions—but free.

The Shemitah is a reminder that God is the source of all blessings, spiritual and physical alike. But when God is removed from the picture, the removal of blessings will ultimately follow. The Shemitah thus deals with a particular flaw of human nature—the tendency to divorce the blessings of life from the Giver of those blessings, to separate the physical realm from the spiritual realm, and then compensate for the loss of the spiritual by increasing its claims over the physical world—pursuing more and more things, increase, gain—materialism. This increase of things, in turn, further crowds out the presence of God. The Shemitah is the antidote to all these things—the clearing away of material attachments to allow the work and presence of God to come in.

The observance of the Shemitah is an act of submission and humility. It is the acknowledgment that every good thing comes from God and cannot ultimately be owned, only received as an entrustment. Possessions are let go, accounts are wiped out, that which has built up is wiped away. The Shemitah humbles the pride of man.

Lastly, the Shemitah shares the attributes of the Sabbath day—an entire year given to rest and let rest, to release and be released, to unburden others and lay one's burdens down, to wipe clean the slate and have one's own slate wiped clean—the time appointed by God for rest, refreshing, and revival.

First Puzzle Pieces

Before we move on, let's take stock of what we now know about the first key. These are the puzzle pieces that will become critical to unlock the mystery of the Shemitah:

- The Shemitah is to years what the Sabbath is to days.
- It takes place once every seven years.
- It is unique and distinct from the six years that precede it.
- It is the year of cessation, release, and rest—the ceasing of what has not ceased up to the time of its coming.
- The Shemitah specifically touches the financial and economic realms.
- It leads and builds up to its climactic final day, Elul 29, the Day of Remission, the Day of Nullification.

- On Elul 29, all debts are canceled and all credit released, and the nation's financial accounts are transformed and wiped clean.

- The Shemitah is sweeping, radical, and extreme.

- Its effects, consequences, and repercussions bear key similarities to that of a financial and economic collapse.

The Shemitah, like the Sabbath day, was intended to be a blessing for the nation of Israel. The words and concepts most associated with it—"the release," "the remission," "the forgiveness of debt"—are all positive. But the mystery of the Shemitah concerns judgment. This raises an important and obvious question: How could something intended to be a national blessing become linked to national judgment?

Let's take it one step further: How could something intended to be a national blessing transform into national judgment? In the next chapter we will find the second key to the answer.

Chapter 5

SECOND KEY: 586 BC
and the JUDGMENT SIGN

The Prophet in the Ruins

How lonely sits the city that was full of people! How like
a widow is she, who was great among the nations!...All
her gates are desolate...Her children have gone into
captivity...

—LAMENTATIONS 1:1–5

THE PROPHET WALKS in the midst of the ruins of the fallen city. What was once the capital of his nation, the city of kings and princes, now lies in ashes and rubble. The streets are desolate. The city upon which rested the name and glory of God is destroyed. The land of Zion is left desolate.

He had not been silent. He had sounded the alarm and warned his nation, over and over and over again. But they had rejected the warning and the bearer of that warning. They persecuted him and placed him in prison. And then the calamity of which he had long prophesied finally happened. The kingdom was no more. Gone was the Temple. Gone were the priests. Gone was the nation he had known and loved.

The year was 586 BC. The city was Jerusalem. The kingdom was Judah. And the prophet was named "Yirmayahu" or, as he would later be known to much of the world, Jeremiah. He wept not only for the city and the land but also for his people. The city was desolate. Its fields were abandoned. Men, women, and children were taken captive into exile in the land of those who had wrought the destruction. Now, by the rivers of Babylon, they sat down and wept.

The Mystery of the Seventy Years

Jeremiah had prophesied all of it, the destruction and the exile. In fact, the Lord had revealed to him the length of the judgment, the exact number of years:

> And the LORD has sent to you all His servants the prophets...but you have not listened nor inclined your ear to hear. They said, "Repent now everyone of his evil way and his evil doings, and dwell in the land that the LORD has given to you and your fathers forever and ever... Therefore thus says the LORD of hosts: 'Because

you have not heard My words...this whole land shall
be a desolation and an astonishment, and these nations
shall serve the king of Babylon seventy years.'"
—JEREMIAH 25:4–11

According to Jeremiah's prophecy, for seventy years the
nation would be under the dominion of Babylon. At the end
of the appointed time the Lord would cause Babylon to fall
and the exiles to return to Zion. The prophecy would come
true in 539 BC with the fall of the Babylonian Empire and the
rise of the Persians led by King Cyrus. Cyrus would issue a
decree granting the exiled Jewish people the right to return
and rebuild their land. But why seventy years? The reason is
deeply rooted in a mystery more ancient still.

"As Long as She Lay Desolate"

The Book of 2 Chronicles sheds more light on the same
destruction and exile of which Jeremiah prophesied:

And the LORD God of their fathers sent warnings to them
by His messengers...But they mocked the messengers of
God, despised His words, and scoffed at His prophets,
until the wrath of the LORD arose against His people, till
there was no remedy. Therefore He brought against them
the king of the Chaldeans...They burned the house of
God, broke down the wall of Jerusalem, burned all its
palaces with fire...
—2 CHRONICLES 36:15–19

The account goes on to speak of those carried away into
exile. And then the missing key appears:

And those who escaped from the sword he carried away
to Babylon, where they became servants to him and his

sons until the rule of the kingdom of Persia, to fulfill the
word of the LORD by the mouth of Jeremiah, *until the
land had enjoyed her Sabbaths. As long as she lay desolate she kept Sabbath, to fulfill seventy years.*
—2 CHRONICLES 36:20–21,
EMPHASIS ADDED

"Until the land had enjoyed her Sabbaths" is a very strange
and striking statement. How does a land enjoy its Sabbaths?
And what could this possibly have to do with the seventy years
of judgment? The answer is found in the deserts of Sinai.

The Torah Clue

In Leviticus 26 a prophecy is given of what would happen to
the people of Israel if they turned away from God. They would
be removed from the land and scattered to the nations. The
prophecy would come true in 586 BC with the destruction of
Jerusalem. But it is here in the Torah that the vital connection
is revealed:

I will lay your cities waste and bring your sanctuaries to
desolation…I will bring the land to desolation…your
land shall be desolate and your cities waste. *Then the
land shall enjoy its sabbaths as long as it lies desolate
and you are in your enemies' land; then the land shall
rest and enjoy its sabbaths. As long as it lies desolate it
shall rest—for the time it did not rest on your sabbaths
when you dwelt in it.*
—LEVITICUS 26:31–35,
EMPHASIS ADDED

The "sabbaths" of the land referred to in this passage are the
Sabbath years—the Shemitahs. In other words, the Shemitah

would hold the key to the timing of the Lord's judgments. But why and how?

The Covenant Sign

The Shemitah was a sign of the nation's covenant with God. Everything they had, the land and all its blessings, was dependent on that covenant and their relationship with God. It was all entrusted to them, but it belonged to God. If they turned away from God, then their blessings would be removed, or rather, they would be removed from their blessings.

So for the people of Israel to keep the Sabbath year was to acknowledge God's sovereignty over their land and lives. It was also an act of faith. It required their total trust in God's faithfulness to provide for their needs while they ceased from farming. In the same way, to cancel all the debts owed them was to sacrifice monetary gain and, again, to rely on God's providence.

Lastly, the keeping of the Shemitah was, above all, an act of devotion and worship, to put God above everything else in one's life. But for all this, a blessing was promised. If Israel would keep the Shemitah, God would keep and bless Israel with all that was needed and beyond.

The Broken Shemitah

On the other hand, to abandon or reject the Shemitah would signify the opposite—the breaking of the covenant and the rejection of God's sovereignty over the land and lives. It would be as if they said, "The land does not belong to God, but to us. Our blessings, our possessions, everything we have in our lives, comes not from God but from the work of our hands, nor does it belong to God, but to us. We will not sacrifice profit or gain for the sake of pursuing God, nor will we allow anything to halt or interrupt these pursuits. We have no need, no time, and no room for God in our lives or in the life of our nation."

So the matter of the Shemitah was critical. Upon it rested the nation's future.

The Shemitah and the Fall of a Nation

Israel's rejection of the Shemitah set in motion a series of far-reaching consequences and repercussions. If God is not sovereign over the land and its people, then the land and its people become cut off from the Creator. A God-centered worldview is replaced by a man-centered and self-centered worldview. So the people of Israel drove God out of their lives to become their own gods, masters of the land, their world, and their destiny. They could now rewrite the law and redefine what was right and wrong, moral and immoral.

Without God nothing would be holy or, for that matter, unholy. Nothing had any purpose except the purpose they now assigned it. And with no true purpose, they could do whatever they wanted—not only with their land but also with their lives, with each other, and with their children. Thus they lifted up their children as sacrifices on the altars of foreign gods.

It was for this last transgression that the judgment finally fell. It began with the breaking of the Shemitah and ended in the offering of their sons and daughters in the fires of Baal and Molech, the sin that would bring about the nation's destruction.

The Shemitah's Judgment

When the judgment fell in 586 BC, the holy city would be left a burning ruin, the holy land a vast desolation, and the people captives in a foreign land. What does this have to do with the Shemitah?

The nation had driven God out of their lives and the Shemitah from their land. Now it would return to them. What they had refused to observe freely would now come upon them by force. It would come back at them not in the form of blessing, but of judgment.

They had driven the Shemitah from the land. Now the Shemitah had returned, and they themselves were driven out. They had removed God from their lives. Now their blessings would likewise be removed from their lives, and their lives from their blessings.

The Shemitah's Desolations

During the Shemitah there was to be no sowing or reaping of the land. The nation had rejected the ordinance and had worked the land continuously, exploiting it for gain. But when the Shemitah returned to the land in the form of judgment, all sowing and reaping ceased, all tending of vineyards and groves came to an end, and no one worked the land. Through judgment and calamity the ordinance was now fulfilled.

During the Shemitah everyone who owned a vineyard or a grove had to open it up to those in need. Every field had to now be accessible to the poor. The gates of walled and fenced lands were unlocked and left open the entire year. In the destruction of 586 BC the gates were opened by force, walls were broken down, fences were destroyed, vineyards were exposed, groves were left unprotected, and private land became public and accessible to all. In judgment the Shemitah was fulfilled.

On the Shemitah's last and climactic day all debt was canceled, all credit annulled, and the nation's financial accounts were transformed in a massive nullification. In 586 BC the nation's financial accounts were, likewise, transformed in a massive wiping away of the nation's financial realm. The calamity canceled and wiped out debt and nullified credit by force. As it had always done, the Shemitah had transformed the nation's financial realm, only now by the force of destruction.

The effect of the Shemitah was to wipe away that which had been built up. In 586 BC the Shemitah wiped away the kingdom itself. That which had been built up, the nation's palaces and towers, were all wiped away. The kingdom itself had been nullified.

The Severe Sabbath

The Shemitah was the Sabbath of years, the year of rest, of fallow ground, of unkept vineyards, of stillness. In 586 BC and the years that followed, with the people in exile, the land of Israel rested. Its fields lay fallow, its groves unkept, its vineyards untended, its threshing floors silent, its olive trees abandoned, and its vine presses still. What was ordained from Sinai was now fulfilled:

> Then the land shall enjoy its sabbaths as long as it lies desolate and you are in your enemies' land; then the land shall rest and enjoy its sabbaths.
> —Leviticus 26:34

There had been a total of seventy Sabbath or Shemitah years that the nation had not observed. So Israel's judgment would last seventy years.

> As long as it lies desolate it shall rest—for the time it did not rest on your Sabbaths when you dwelt in it.
> —Leviticus 26:35

So it was the mystery of the Shemitah that held the secret of the timing of the nation's judgment.

The Shemitah and World History

The judgment that fell on the land of Israel in 586 BC was a pivotal event in biblical history, Jewish history, and world history. In it the Temple of Jerusalem would be destroyed and the words of the Hebrew prophets fulfilled. In it the Diaspora, the scattering of the Jewish people throughout the world, would begin and the stage set for the formation of what would be known as Judaism and the coming of a Jewish rabbi named Yeshua or Jesus, whose life would irrevocably change the history of the world.

And behind it all was the mystery of the Shemitah. In other words, this obscure, little known, ancient mystery has already affected the entire planet and those who live on it in ways too vast to measure.

_____

But could there be more to it? Could the mystery of the Shemitah still be at work—moving, impacting, and altering the course of world history—even in the modern world, even in our day?

If so, what form would it take on? How would the Shemitah manifest in the modern world? For the answer, another key is needed.

Chapter 6

THIRD KEY:
The PROPHETIC MANIFESTATION

What If the Mystery Was Still in Effect?

ACCORDING TO THE Book of 2 Chronicles, the mystery of the Shemitah was operating behind one of the most pivotal events in world history, the destruction of the kingdom in 586 BC. But what if the mystery was still in effect? Or what if it was to manifest again in the modern world? What if it was operating right now, still touching, affecting, determining, or altering the course of human history in modern times? What would that look like?

The Shemitah's Economic Connection

In modern economies a very small percentage of people work the land, gather in harvests, or tend vineyards. So how could the Shemitah break the barrier to operate in the modern world? What happens if we look at the effects and consequences of the Shemitah in purely technical and general terms?

The result is not only relevant but also surprisingly applicable to our day: the effect and repercussions of the Shemitah extend into the nation's financial realm, economic realm, and the realms of labor, employment, production, consumption, and trade.

Though most modern economies are not centered on agriculture but are industrial or postindustrial, all of these attributes still apply. Thus if the Shemitah was to manifest in modern times, it would affect a nation's financial realm, its economic realm, and its realms of labor, employment, production, consumption, and trade.

Economic Collapse

Over the course of the Shemitah the nation's production is severely decreased. For a modern nation to witness a severe decreasing of its production would point to an economic downturn or recession, an economic collapse, or a depression. During such times demand dries up, corporations downsize, factories cut back on output, and businesses close their doors.

During the Shemitah the nation's labor is greatly reduced or comes to a cessation. In the case of a modern nation this would translate to massive unemployment. All of these, again, are characteristics of an economic recession or depression.

During the Shemitah the buying and selling of the land's produce are restricted and the fruits of labor are abandoned. Here we have yet another characteristic of economic recessions and collapses. Demand dries up. Consumption plunges. Commerce dwindles. Consumers cut back on their spending. Merchandise sits untouched in stores and warehouses, and international trade suffers massive declines. The fruits and products of the nation's industry and services are abandoned.

Financial Collapse

On its climactic day, Elul 29, the force of the Shemitah causes credit to be canceled and debt to be wiped away. The nation's financial accounts are transformed, nullified, and wiped clean.

The description again points us to an economic implosion and, more specifically, to a financial collapse. Such collapses produce corporate failures, bank failures, foreclosures, and bankruptcies. Debt and credit are nullified. And in financial crises involving stock market crashes, financial accounts are transformed, nullified, and wiped clean. Billions of dollars are wiped away in a matter of hours or minutes.

The effects and consequences of the Shemitah consistently point in the direction of a specific event—an economic and financial collapse. This resemblance of the Shemitah to an economic implosion has been noted even by the rabbis.

The Shemitah: Observances and Cataclysms

On one hand, we have the Shemitah as a biblically ordained occurrence, a religious event, a Sabbath rest, and a blessing, carried out through the voluntary observance of God's people. On the other hand, we have the destruction of a kingdom— an event that comes about through a multitude of causes entirely from having nothing to do with a voluntarily religious observance. How can the two be connected? The Bible itself establishes the connection in Leviticus 26, when it speaks of a military invasion of such magnitude that it reduces entire cities to ruins and the land to a depopulated devastation—and yet it speaks of the land's desolation as a fulfillment of the Shemitah.

The Shemitah in Modern Translation

So regardless of the means by which it comes, the ultimate result is the same. It is the *effect* of the Shemitah that manifests, whether through the voluntary observance of God's people or by a calamitous event. The sowers and reapers of ancient Israel were to voluntarily cease from working for the duration of the Shemitah; in the modern world, economic downturns and implosions force people from employment and labor. The means are different—but the end result is the same.

In the ancient Shemitah, the voluntary abandoning of fields and groves meant that the land's yield and productivity plummeted; in the modern world, the plummeting of production and yield are caused by economic collapses. In the ancient Shemitah, the people were not to buy, sell, or partake in the fruit of the land; in the modern world, economic collapses cause the plunging of consumption and trade. And in the ancient Shemitah, the people were to wipe clean their financial accounts by canceling out debt and credit; in the modern world, financial collapses cause credit to fail, debts to go unpaid, and financial accounts to be wiped out.

Sowing and Reaping in the Modern World

It is striking to note how many agricultural terms connected with the Shemitah are also linked to the economic and financial realms. Financial investment is called "sowing." The funding given to launch a financial enterprise is called "seed money." The starting of a new enterprise is called "planting." When a financial investment produces returns, those returns are called the "yield." This yield is part of its coming to "fruition." One then "reaps" the yield.

The connection is just as strong in the ancient Hebrew. In one of the ordinances of the Shemitah it is written:

> And if you say, "What shall we eat in the seventh year, since we shall not sow nor gather in our *produce*?"
>
> —LEVITICUS 25:20,
>
> *EMPHASIS ADDED*

Behind the English word *produce* is the Hebrew *tebuah*. *Tebuah* can be translated as "fruit" and "produce," but also as "gain," "income," and "revenue."

Here, as before, we find the connection of the Shemitah to the economic realm. The Shemitah impacts a nation's material blessings, that which makes up its prosperity, its productivity, and its sustenance. In modern nations that translates to the economic and financial realms. So if the Shemitah was to operate in the modern world, we would expect it to be especially linked to those same realms. And since the nature of the Shemitah is to bring about cessation, this would translate to an economic or financial collapse.

The Shemitah as a Prophetic Sign

But can the manifestation of the Shemitah go even further? Can it extend beyond the economic realm? Can it manifest in other forms of cessation, collapse, or even destruction? The answer is found in the account of 2 Chronicles concerning the calamity that fell upon the land in 586 BC. According to the account, the Babylonian invasion of the land, the burning of

Jerusalem, the exile of the people from the land, are all a part of the manifesting of the Shemitah.

This presents a jarring fusion. On one hand is the Shemitah, a religious observance of rest, the Sabbath year. On the other hand is a national cataclysm that sets a city on fire and wipes away an entire kingdom. The one is all about release, the other—a nation taken by force into captivity and exile.

How do these two jarring realities go together? The answer is they don't go together. They are one and the same. According to the account, that which fell upon the land of Israel in 586 BC was not just connected to the Shemitah—it *was* the Shemitah.

> As long as she lay desolate she kept Sabbath...
> —2 CHRONICLES 36:21

The destruction was the Shemitah. All the unkept, unobserved, and unfulfilled Shemitahs from Israel's past were now returning to find their fulfillment. The seventy years of judgment *were* the seventy unkept Shemitahs from Israel's past. The Shemitah had returned in an altered form. It had transformed. It was now operating through conflict and war, political alliances, the deportation and exile of an entire people, and the countless variables of human actions, reactions, and interactions.

The Shemitah and the Two Empires

The Shemitah lay behind the march of Babylonian armies into the Promised Land, the burning of the Temple, the removal of the people from the land, and their years in exile. It operated on an epic scale, transcending the boundaries of ancient Israel and involving foreign peoples, nations, and empires.

In order for the land to rest and keep its missing Sabbaths, the Jewish people had to be removed from the land. In order for the Jewish people to be removed from the land, the Babylonian Empire had to ascend onto the world stage. In order for the Babylonian Empire to ascend, the Assyrian Empire had to fall.

Once the land kept its Sabbaths, the Babylonian captivity could come to an end. In order for that to happen, another empire had to rise—that of Persia. Thus the Babylonian Empire happens to rise at the time that the seventy years of the Shemitah must commence. Then when the seventy years of Shemitah are complete, it falls. It falls because the empire of Persia rises. Thus the Persian Empire happens to rise at the same time the Shemitahs draw to their end. The mystery of the Shemitah thus becomes global, affecting the course of nations beyond and far removed from Israel and causing the rise and fall of powers, kingdoms, and world empires.

The Shemitah as a Pattern

Does the mystery of the Shemitah always involve judgment? Not necessarily. Nor is it a simplistic equation whereby every manifestation can neatly be attributed to a particular sin. And as we have seen, the same manifestation can mean the fall of one power and the rise of another. The Shemitah forms an underlying pattern and dynamic that, given the right circumstances, will manifest in a specific way. Its manifestations may vary in form but will exhibit consistent characteristics, operate through a consistent dynamic, and produce consistent repercussions.

Given the circumstance of a nation or civilization, dedicated from its inception to the will of God but now in departure from that will, in defiance of His ways and at war with

His sovereignty, as it was with ancient Israel, the Shemitah will increasingly, more intensely, and more severely manifest in the direction of judgment.

What Would Shemitah Look Like Today?

At the beginning of this chapter I posed a question as to what the mystery of the Shemitah would look like if it was operating in the modern world. To now answer that question, let us assemble the pieces of the puzzle.

The Overall Manifestation

- The Shemitah declares God's sovereignty, dominion, and ownership over all things.
- It specifically touches the realm of a nation's prosperity and sustenance.
- It manifests as the Sabbath year and is distinct from the six years preceding it.
- It bears witness that all blessings come from God.
- It humbles the pride of man.
- It lays bare man's total dependence on God.
- It separates wealth and possessions from the owner.
- It wipes away that which has built up in the previous years.
- It levels imbalance and erases accounts.
- It causes cessation, pauses, interruptions, and endings.
- It reveals the link between the physical, material realm and the spiritual realm.
- It bears witness against materialism.

- It calls the nation to turn away from material pursuits and to the spiritual.

- It releases entanglements, attachments, and bondages.

- It brings about rest—Sabbath.

- It calls the nation back to God.

The Economic Manifestation

- The Shemitah carries a special connection to and bears special consequence on a nation's economic realm.

- Its effect and repercussions extend into the realms of labor, production, employment, revenue, consumption, trade, and finance.

- It causes production to cease or severely decrease.

- It causes labor to cease or be greatly reduced.

- It causes the private realm to increasingly yield to the public realm, and private ownership to be increasingly subject to public necessities.

- It causes buying and selling, the transactions of commerce, to be greatly curtailed.

- It builds up to its peak day, the Day of Remission, on Elul 29.

- It causes a nation's financial accounts to be transformed, annulled, and wiped clean.

- It causes credit to be unpaid and debt released. Credit and debt are wiped away.

- It acts as an economic and financial leveler, wiping out that which has been allowed to build up in the preceding years, nullifying imbalance.

- It erases accounts and causes release and remission in the economic and financial realms.

The Prophetic Manifestation

The Shemitah is also a prophetic sign of national judgment...

- To a nation that has rejected the sovereignty of God, a nation that no longer sees itself as "under God."

- To a nation that has driven God out of its culture.

- To a nation that has divorced its blessings from the hand of God.

- To a nation that pursues increase and prosperity above righteousness and over God.

- To a nation that seeks material blessing or pleasure as an end, in and of itself.

- To a nation that once knew God but has now largely forgotten Him.

- To a nation that once knew the ways of God but now rejects them.

- Upon a nation that specifically strikes that nation's blessings, prosperity, and sustenance.

- That bears witness to that nation that all of its blessings come from God, and without Him those blessings cannot remain but will be removed.

- That bears witness against that nation's materialism.
- That strikes the nation's economic realm.
- That wipes out the nation's financial accounts.
- That humbles the nation and casts down its objects of pride and glory.
- That separates wealth and possessions from that nation.
- That causes cessation, pauses, interruptions, and endings.
- That releases entanglements, attachments, and bondages among the people of the nation.
- That lays bare the nation's total dependence on God.
- That holds the key to the specific timing of national judgment.
- That directs the nation away from the worldly and the material.
- That calls the nation back to God.

The Global Manifestation

The Shemitah, in its most far-reaching manifestation…

- Operates on an epic and global scale, transcending national borders and involving every realm of life.
- Involves not only the economic and financial realm but also the political realm, the cultural realm, the sociological realm, the military realm, and even the natural realm.

- Though directly impacting the financial and economic realms, its outworking can be triggered or accompanied by events of entirely different realms.

- Can manifest in the form of a cataclysmic event.

- Can wipe away not only financial accounts but also physical realities—buildings, walls, towers, and cities.

- Can alter the landscape of nations and powers.

- Can involve and affect the rise and fall of great powers and determine the course of empires.

———————

We have now identified the dynamics and nature of the Shemitah as a pattern and template as well as a sign of national judgment. But one question remains. In ancient times, the focal point of the Shemitah was the nation and land of Israel. If the Shemitah was to manifest in the modern world, on what stage would it operate? Where would it play out?

To answer that question, we will need one more clue...

Chapter 7

FOURTH KEY:
The SECRET ISRAEL

Beyond 586 BC

IN ITS FIRST and original context the Shemitah is connected to Israel. It is the only nation commanded to observe it. And, as we have seen, it is still kept, in varying degrees, by the observants of that nation. But we are not dealing here with the Shemitah as an observance but as a prophetic sign—particularly as a warning or manifestation of national judgment.

Such a prophetic sign could be given to any nation as long as that nation in some way matched the description or shared the attributes of ancient Israel in 586 BC. In other words, it would have to be:

- A nation warranting a prophetic warning or man-ifestation of judgment, a nation in defiance of God's ways

This description could, to varying degrees, fit much of the world's nations—whether religious or secular, Hindu, Muslim, Christian, or communist. Let's narrow it down further with a more specific description:

- A nation that had once known God, but had now turned away from Him and rejected His ways

This description could match several of the world's Western nations, formerly seen as "Christian" but now largely post-Christian. Let's narrow it down still further:

- A civilization established on the Word of God, dedicated to His purposes, and consecrated to His glory from its very inception

Now the field of candidates is severely reduced. It can be argued that only two civilizations in human history were estab-lished, dedicated, and consecrated to the will, the word, the purposes, and the glory of God from the moment of their con-ceptions. The first was Israel; the second was America.

American civilization was established and dedicated at Cape Henry, Plymouth, and Massachusetts Bay to the purposes of God.

The Israel of the New World

But let's take it even further:

- A civilization specifically established after the pattern of ancient Israel

Most would find it surprising to learn that America was consciously, intentionally, and specifically founded and formed after the pattern of ancient Israel. Its founders saw it as a new Israel, the Israel of the New World. It was their exodus from Europe like the Hebrew exodus from Egypt. The New World was their new promised land, and the Massachusetts Bay Colony was their New Jerusalem.

As for the legal system of the new American commonwealth, the Puritans sought to incorporate the Law of Moses. They instituted a day of rest after the pattern of the Hebrew Sabbath. And the American holiday, Thanksgiving, was formed after the pattern of the Hebrew Sukkot, the Feast of Tabernacles.

They named the mountains of America after the mountains of Israel: Mount Gilead, Mount Hermon, Mount Ephraim, Mount Moriah, Mount Carmel, and Mount Zion. They called their towns and cities, Jericho, Jordan, Salem, Canaan, Goshen, Hebron, and Beersheba. They named their children Joshua, Rachel, Ezra, Zechariah, Esther, Jeremiah, and a host of other names derived from the people of ancient Israel.

They even taught Hebrew in their schools and universities. On the seal of Yale University appear the Hebrew words from the breastplate of the high priest. On the seal of Columbia University appears the ancient Hebrew name for God. And on the seal of Dartmouth University appear the Hebrew words translating to "the Almighty God."

America's link to ancient Israel has undergirded its national identity, in one form or another, consciously or unconsciously, from the time of its inception onward. It is clearly evident at the time of American independence when Benjamin Franklin proposed that the new nation's Great Seal should feature the image of Moses parting the Red Sea, while Thomas Jefferson proposed that of the Israelites journeying through the wilderness.[1]

The connection is unique, deep, and intrinsic. The pattern of ancient Israel is embedded in the DNA of American civilization. It's in the root from which America sprang. One observer wrote this:

> No Christian community in history identified more with
> the People of the Book than did the early settlers of the
> Massachusetts Bay Colony, who believed their own lives
> to be a literal reenactment of the Biblical drama of the
> Hebrew nation.[2]

There is no nation in the modern world so deeply linked to ancient Israel as America. There is, therefore, no stage or platform on earth so well suited for the manifesting of the mystery of the Shemitah as America. Is the Israel connection necessary for the mystery to manifest? No. It could manifest to any nation, just as God could send a warning of national judgment to any nation. No unique connection to ancient Israel is needed for America to be given a biblical sign of national judgment. But the fact that America does bear such a deep connection to ancient Israel makes it all the more striking and fitting for the same signs used to warn Israel of judgment to warn America.

The Fall of Ancient Israel

But a key factor is still missing: Why would the sign of the Shemitah, an ancient portent of judgment, be given to America in the first place? The answer lies in a metamorphosis that began thousands of years before America was born.

Israel was unique among the nations of the ancient world. No nation had ever been brought into existence so directly connected to the purposes and promises of God. No nation had ever been given a divine revelation as that which was given to Israel on Mount Sinai. No nation had ever seen the hand of God so directly affecting its course as had Israel. And no nation had ever been joined to God in a national covenant.

But at the peak of its blessings a metamorphosis began. The nation began turning away from the God of their foundation. The change was subtle at first but, in time, grew more and more blatant and brazen. Whether by conscious intent or unconscious abandonment, the people began driving God out of their lives, out of their culture, out of their government, and out of the instruction of their children. In His place they brought in idols and foreign gods, and in place of His ways they now followed the ways of the pagan nations that surrounded them.

They redefined what was right and wrong. They created a new morality to replace the old. They called evil "good," and good "evil." What they had once celebrated, they now condemned, and what they once worshipped, they now reviled. On the other hand, what they had once condemned, they now celebrated, and what they had once reviled, they now worshipped. They grew increasingly carnal, materialistic, sexually immoral, and self-indulgent, and their culture, likewise, grew increasingly coarse and vulgar. And then, as did the nations surrounding them, they began to lift up their children as sacrifices on the altars of their new gods.

As for those in their midst who refused to go along with their moral and spiritual apostasy, those who remained faithful to God and His ways, they were now marginalized, mocked,

vilified, and, finally, persecuted. The nation that had been
brought into existence to be a vessel of God's purposes had
now transformed into its very opposite—a civilization turned
in upon itself, at war against its own foundations, and at war
with God.

This is the setting and the stage, the nation to which the
warnings, the signs, the harbingers, and manifestations of
national judgment are sent—one of which is the sign of the
Shemitah.

The Fall of the Second Israel

What about America? What happened to the civilization so
uniquely joined from its foundation to ancient Israel?

America's founders prophesied that inasmuch as the new
civilization would follow the ways of God, it would be blessed
with the blessings given to Israel. And what they foretold came
true. America became the most blessed nation on earth. By
the twentieth century it had become the most prosperous, the
most secure, the most revered, and the most powerful nation
on earth.

But at the pinnacle of its power and the height of its prosperity relative to the rest of the world, a metamorphosis began.
The "Israel of the New World" would reenact the apostasy and
fall of the Israel of the ancient world. America now began a
progression that would end with the nation's turning away
from the God of its foundation.

The metamorphosis was subtle at first but, in time, would
grow more and more blatant and brazen. As did ancient Israel,
so now America began removing God from its national life,
from its culture, its government, and its public squares. It would
ban prayer and the reading of Scripture from the instruction of
its children. The school system that had come into existence for

the purpose of teaching the Word of God would now treat that Word as contraband. And as America eliminated the presence of God from its national life and culture, it filled the void with idols and formed gods out of its desires.

As did ancient Israel, America progressively redefined what was right and wrong, adopting a new morality to replace the old. It now called evil "good," and good "evil." What it had once celebrated, it now condemned, and what it had once worshipped, it now reviled. And on the other hand, what it had once condemned, it now celebrated and what it had once reviled, it now worshipped. American culture grew increasingly carnal, materialistic, coarse, vulgar, and self-indulgent.

Instead of being "a light to the world" as its founders had envisioned, America was now saturating the world with pornography. And while Israel had killed thousands of its children on the altars of its new gods, America killed not thousands but millions of its unborn children on the altars of its pleasures and convenience. Its collective hands were covered in blood.

As for those within America who refused to go along with its moral and spiritual apostasy, those who remained faithful to God and His ways, they were now increasingly marginalized in the nation's newly apostate culture, mocked in its media, vilified in its public discourse, and increasingly in danger of persecution.

America, brought into existence and dedicated by its founders to be a vessel of God's purposes, had now transformed into its very opposite: a civilization turned in upon itself, at war against its own foundations, and at war with God.

Those who founded America not only foretold its future blessings—but also gave warning. It was this: if America ever turned away from God, then the same judgments that fell upon ancient Israel would fall upon America.[3] The appearance of the same harbingers in America that had once appeared in the last days of ancient Israel matches their prophecies.

The Shemitah and the Nations

So we now have the missing key—a civilization uniquely joined to the pattern of ancient Israel but now undergoing the same apostasy that brought the ancient nation into judgment and destruction—a nation that had once known God but had now not only turned *away* from Him but also *against* Him. It was this scenario that, in ancient times, invoked the judgment of the Shemitah.

Added to this is America's place among the nations. In modern times America has occupied the center stage of world history as the greatest economic, financial, military, political, and cultural power on earth. That alone would give it a central place in the mystery.

On the other hand, though America is central to the mystery, it is not alone in the mystery. The issue of judgment and the specific judgments revealed in this book concern all nations and peoples—for several reasons:

- First, because of its centrality, what happens to America affects the rest of the world.

- Second, the sins and immoralities that echo the sins of ancient Israel are shared by many nations beyond American shores.

- Third, the overall setting for Israel's judgment—a civilization that had once known the ways of God but now is in defiance of God and His ways—is shared by other nations other than America.

- Fourth, though the Shemitah may focus on specific nations, its effects are far-reaching and transcend geography and the borders of nations.

We now have the stage. The mystery will touch America, but its effect will not be confined to America. Its consequences and repercussions will touch the entire world. Having located the place of the mystery, one last clue is needed to reveal the time.

Chapter 8

FIFTH KEY:
The TISHRI CONNECTION

The Most Holy of Months

THE HOLIEST MONTH on the biblical Hebrew calendar is that of *Tishri*. On the Western calendar Tishri falls in the period between September and October. It is so sacred a month that ten of its days are known as "the High Holy Days." Every Hebrew month begins with the day or night of the new moon.

But the month of Tishri is so sacred that the day on which it begins, its new moon is itself a high holy day. Most Hebrew months contain none of the sacred appointed holy days given at Sinai. But Tishri contains ten of them, not including at least nine other days also deemed as holy.

Hebrew Month of Tishri

Seventh Month of the Sacred Calendar—
First Month of the Civil Calendar

Feast of Trumpets	Days of Awe	Days of Awe	Days of Awe	Days of Awe	Days of Awe	Days of Awe	Days of Awe	Days of Awe	Yom Kippur					Sukkot	Sukkot	Sukkot	Sukkot	Sukkot	Sukkot	Sukkot	Shemini Atzeret							
1	2	3	4	5	6	7	8	9	10	11	12	13	14	15	16	17	18	19	20	21	22	23	24	25	26	27	28	30

Thus there is no month in the biblical year like Tishri. What are its themes, its meaning, and its message?

The Time of Judgment

The rabbis saw Tishri and the high holy days of autumn as focusing on the kingship of God, His rule, His power, His sovereignty, and His dominion. The sounding of the shofars during the Feast of Trumpets was, among other things, the proclaiming of the Lord as King and Sovereign over the world, over the nation, and over the lives of His people.

The month of Tishri is also known as the time of judgment. Its opening day, the Feast of Trumpets, is also known as *Yom Ha Din*, or "the Day of Judgment." During the Feast of Trumpets the shofars are sounded. The sound of the shofar is not only that of a solemn gathering but is the sound of alarm and warning, the harbinger of approaching danger, the warning of impending judgment. Tishri is the month of reckoning, when the nation stands before God and when sin is dealt with.

The Time of Teshuvah

In view of the judgment associated with its coming, Tishri has become the month of repentance. The "Ten Days of Awe" with which the month begins are also called "The Days of Teshuvah." *Teshuvah* is the Hebrew word for repentance. It comes from the root word *shuv*, which means "to turn." The Days of Awe were given for the purpose of turning the course of one's life, forgiving and being forgiven, repenting of one's sins, withdrawing from worldly pursuits, and doing whatever was needed to get right with man and God.

The Shemitah-Tishri Connection

The themes of Tishri match the themes of the Shemitah. Both speak of God's sovereignty. Both are linked to judgment. Both call the nation to return to God. Both are linked to nullification, cancellation, and release—one concerning sin and the other concerning debt. The Shemitah is the seventh year. Tishri is the seventh month.

The Beginning and the End

Ancient Israel reckoned time by two different calendars: the sacred calendar and the civil calendar. The sacred calendar began in the springtime, in the month of Nisan. In the sacred calendar Tishri is the seventh month. But in the civil calendar Tishri is the first month, the beginning of the New Year. Why is this significant?

Elul and Tishri

Elul—Sixth Month of Sacred Year

ELUL												TISHRI									
Days of Repentance	Days of Repentance	Days of Repentance	Days of Repentance	Days of Repentance	Days of Repentance	Days of Repentance	Days of Repentance	Days of Repentance	Days of Repentance	Days of Repentance	Days of Repentance	Feast of Trumpets	Days of Awe	Days of Awe	Days of Awe	Days of Awe	Days of Awe	Days of Awe	Days of Awe	Days of Awe	Yom Kippur
18	19	20	21	22	23	24	25	26	27	28	29	1	2	3	4	5	6	7	8	9	10

The Shemitah was based on the civil calendar. Thus the Shemitah year always began with the month of Tishri—specifically, it always began with Tishri's first day, which was also the Feast of Trumpets. One year later the Shemitah would end—at sunset on the twenty-ninth day of Elul. But the same sunset that ended Elul 29 would also begin the month of Tishri at the same moment. So the Shemitah year ends the same moment Tishri begins.

Thus Tishri is the Shemitah's key and pivotal month. The Shemitah begins with Tishri at the end of the sixth year and concludes with Tishri at the end of the seventh year. Tishri is the beginning and end of the Shemitah.

The Tishri Key (and Elul)

The Shemitah's greatest impact is manifested at two points—its opening and its closing. Each point coincides with the month of Tishri.

The Shemitah's first point of impact falls on the first day of Tishri at the start of the seventh year. The Shemitah's second point of impact falls at the end of the seventh year when all debts and credits are wiped out. But the exact end of the seventh year comes at nightfall of Elul 29. Thus the moment the sun sets, all debts and credits are reckoned as gone, wiped away—the month of Elul is over and Tishri begins.

So the month of Elul builds up to the Shemitah's two critical points of impact and contains the Shemitah's climactic day. But the month of Tishri, coming immediately after these two critical points of change, most clearly manifests the Shemitah's economic and financial repercussions.

First Impact:
Tishri and the Shemitah's Opening

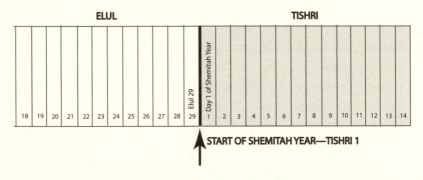

The beginning of the Shemitah is less dramatic than its end as the initial change is simply that of ceasing. The people stop working the land and the fields are abandoned. The effect of this on the land would be less noticeable at the beginning, but increasingly noticeable as the year progressed—and when no harvest appears in the fields.

In pure economic terms this would translate to the beginning of a downturn in a nation's economy—the diminishing of production, consumption, labor, employment, trade, and commerce. The month of Tishri at the beginning of the Shemitah year would be the first to reflect this change and manifest its repercussions. The downward turn in the nation's economic realm would then become more evident in time.

Last Impact:
Tishri and the Shemitah's Climactic End

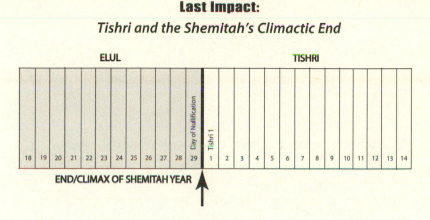

When the sun goes down on Elul 29, all the nation's debts are wiped away as its financial accounts are wiped clean. The same moment marks the start of Tishri. Thus this particular month of Tishri that comes at the end of the Shemitah year most clearly manifests the financial repercussions of that year and of that day.

The Shemitah's Wake:
The Season of Repercussions

The repercussions triggered by the Day of Remission would be most dramatically seen in the ensuing days of Tishri but would not be confined to them. The repercussions would continue into the subsequent month of Heshvan and onward. The entire autumn period at the end of the seventh year is the Shemitah's wake—when these repercussions would be most intensely felt.

Shemitah's Wake

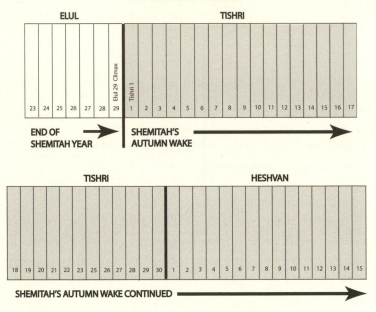

Beyond this, there is nothing confining the repercussions to just one season. They may continue into the winter, the following spring, and onward. But the autumn following the Shemitah's dramatic conclusion, being closest to the Day of Remission, would be foremost in manifesting these repercussions, and within this, Tishri would be foremost.

Elul: The Lead-In Month

We must also take note of the month of Elul. Elul plays a significant role in the Shemitah as well. At the end of the sixth year Elul leads up to the Shemitah's commencement. And at the end of the seventh year Elul leads up to the Shemitah's dramatic end—on Elul 29. Tishri remains the Shemitah's key month, but Elul plays a supporting role as the lead-in month.

The mass wiping clean of a nation's financial accounts would translate into a collapse in the financial realm. Thus if the mystery of the Shemitah is still in effect, we might expect that there exists a connection between the Hebrew month of Tishri and a collapse in the financial realm—as in that of a stock market crash.

Could there exist such a connection? Could an ancient mystery, over three thousand years old, be operating in modern times and even ordaining the fate of world financial markets?

Having now found the fives keys, let us begin to unlock the ancient mystery.

PART III

THE MYSTERY
OF THE SHEMITAH
AND
THE KEY
OF CATACLYSMS

Chapter 9

The FINGERPRINTS of the MYSTERY

The Prophet in the Field

TWO MEN STAND in the midst of vast expanse of farm land. The wind sweeps down on the stalks of wheat, causing a continuously shifting pattern of light and shadow. One of the two, a man named Nouriel, is seeking answers to solve an ancient mystery. The other, in a long dark coat, known only as "the prophet," is seeking to help him do that. The prophet

begins sharing with Nouriel of the ancient observance called
the Shemitah.

The scene just described is from *The Harbinger*. During
this exchange Nouriel asks the prophet a question alluding to
a second mystery. Most people who read the exchange either
missed what was being said or the implications of what was
being said. It was an easy thing to miss as the exchange lasted
just a few lines:

> "How far does the cycle go," I asked, "every seventh year
> in the past…and into the future?"
> "The subject is for another time," he said. "The point
> now is the Shemitah as a sign of judgment."[1]

The prophet had just told Nouriel of the reappearing of the
ancient mystery in modern times, a reappearance linked to the
years 2001 and 2008 and to the nine harbingers of judgment.
Nouriel then asks the prophet if the mystery and its manifestations extend back in time or forward into the future. I included
this exchange from the pages of *The Harbinger* to note that
there was another entire realm to the mystery—but too much
to include in the exchange. The prophet answers Nouriel, "The
subject is for another time." *That time is now.*

Observances vs. Prophetic Signs

Is it possible that the mystery of the Shemitah has been operating in the modern world since before the time of the harbingers? Is it possible that it's been affecting the course of nations
and world history, and that it lies behind some of the most pivotal events of modern times?

To answer this, we must distinguish between the *observance*
of the Shemitah and the Shemitah as a *prophetic sign*. Only

Israel was compelled to keep the Shemitah *as an observance*. As an observance, the Shemitah applies to one nation. But as a prophetic sign, it may apply to any nation. As an observance, the Shemitah comes regularly, every seventh year. But as a sign, it is not bound to any schedule or regularity. But when it does appear, it will manifest the essence of the Shemitah, its effect and mystery, in the form of a sign.

Identifying the Shemitah's Fingerprints

The Shemitah most directly affects and operates within a nation's economic and financial realm. So if the mystery is still in effect, it should be manifesting in these two realms. We must therefore begin our search by looking into the economic and financial realms of the modern world and nations—and specifically in the realm of financial and economic crises, downturns, recessions, depressions, stock market collapses, and crashes.

Since we are not dealing with the command, the observance, and the regulations of the Shemitah, but rather the prophetic signs, we would not expect the manifestation to necessarily occur on a regular basis, every seven years. We would expect rather that it would not be a regular phenomenon but a unique one. We would not expect the connection to be formulaic or simplistic. Nor would we expect that every economic downturn must be connected to the phenomenon. But we will look at the economic downturns, recessions, and depressions of modern times and see if they manifest the fingerprints of the ancient mystery.

Land of Apostasy

In the case of the destruction of Jerusalem in 586 BC, the Shemitah appears as a prophetic sign against a nation in moral

and spiritual apostasy from God. This would point us toward
nations and cultures moving away from their biblical foundations. We have seen that America contains a unique connection to ancient Israel, being formed and established after its
pattern. Therefore while looking at the global picture, and the
nations, we will pay special attention to America.

We will take note that the Shemitah is linked not only to
national judgment but also to national blessing. The sign may
appear at the time of a nation's rise to power. And yet, if that
same nation should turn away from God and the foundations
on which it was established, we would expect the sign of the
Shemitah to increasingly appear as a warning of judgment.

The Clues

We will now see if there could exist any connection between
the occurrences of financial and economic collapses in the
modern world and...

- A seven-year cycle
- The specific seven-year cycle of the biblical Shem-
  itah
- The seventh year of the specific seven-year cycle
- The Hebrew month of Tishri
- Financial or economic collapses and the Hebrew
  month of Tishri converging with the Year of the
  Shemitah
- The autumn wake that seals the end of the sev-
  enth year
- The Hebrew month of Tishri in convergence with
  the Year of the Shemitah

- The Hebrew month of Tishri in convergence with the climactic *end* of the Shemitah year
- The Hebrew month of Elul, or proximity to its point of greatest impact
- The Hebrew month of Heshvan, which begins where Tishri ends

---

Using these keys, we will now open up the backstage of world history. We will look at the greatest economic and financial collapses of modern times. And we will see if the fingerprints of the ancient mystery appear.

Chapter 10

The MYSTERY of SEVEN CRASHES

The Great Crashes

WHAT HAPPENS IF we search for the greatest long-term crashes (as opposed to day crashes) or collapses in stock market history? These will generally be connected to economic crisis and recession. What happens if we take the Bible's ancient mystery of economic cessation and financial nullification and hold it up against these greatest collapses?

The following represent the majority of the greatest long-term stock market crashes in history, arranged in order of increasing magnitude.

The Crash of 2000–2001
The Dot-Com Crash and 9/11

This stock market collapse began with the "Dot-Com Crash" of 2000–2001. Then came 9/11, which would first paralyze Wall Street and then cause further deterioration. The collapse would continue into 2002. By the time it ended, more than 37 percent of the stock market had been wiped out.

Could there be any connection between the crash of 2000 and 2001 and the ancient mystery? The Shemitah comes once every seven years. It just so happens that the first Shemitah of the new millennium fell in the period of 2000–2001, the years of the Dot-Com Crash, a deepening recession, the attack of 9/11, and one of the greatest stock market day crashes in history. The Shemitah year took place entirely within the overall financial and economic collapse. Its overlap with the crash of 2000–2001 is thus 100 percent.

The Crash of 1916–1917
First World War

Also known as the "Crisis of 1916–1917," this stock market crash took place during the First World War. It began in November 1916 and reached its low point one year later in December 1917. What the crash of 1916–1917 lacked in length it made up in severity. By its end, 40 percent of the market had been wiped out.

Could there be any connection between the crash of 1916–1917 and the mystery of the Shemitah? There was one Shemitah in the midst of the First World War. It happened to fall in the years 1916–1917, the same period of the crash. The Shemitah commenced in September 1916. Two months after its beginning, the stock market collapsed. The Shemitah reached its culmination in September 1917 on the Day of Remission. Three months later the collapse was finished. The Shemitah coincided with the economic collapse for ten of its twelve months—an overlap of over 80 percent.

The Crash of 1973
The Crash of Multiple Crises

It began as a currency crisis and was compounded by the 1973 oil crisis and various other national and international crises. By its end, 45 percent of the market had been wiped out. In the two years from 1972 to 1974 the American economy's real gross domestic product (GDP) growth shrank from 7 percent to a negative 2 percent contraction. At the same time inflation soared from a rate of 3 percent in 1972 to 12 percent in 1974. The repercussions of the crash in the United Kingdom were even more dramatic with the London Stock Exchange losing 74 percent of its value and only returning to the same market levels in 1987. Measured in real terms, it would take the United States twenty years to regain the levels lost in this collapse.

Could there be any connection between the crash of 1973 and the ancient mystery? The Shemitah began in the latter part of 1972, with most of its course occurring in 1973. Four months after the Shemitah's beginning, the stock market began to collapse. One of the Shemitah's definitions and consequences is that it causes the nation's production to decrease. The GDP represents the nation's domestic product or production. As the 1972–1973 Shemitah progressed, the nation's domestic production began to fall. By the end of the collapse it had shrunk by 70 percent. The Shemitah took place simultaneously with the collapse in the financial realm for eight of its twelve months—an overlap of over 66 percent.

The Crash of 1901–1903
The Struggle of Titans

The crash of 1901–1903 was brought on by the struggles of E. H. Harriman, Jacob Schiff, and J. P. Morgan to gain financial control of Northern Pacific Railroad. It caused so much damage that the resulting crisis is sometimes called "the 1901–1903 depression." By its end, 46 percent of the market was wiped out.

In the midst and depths of the collapse is the biblical Year of the Shemitah, which began in September 1902 and ended on September 21, 1903. Less than two months after its end, the collapse reached its end. The Shemitah's entire course took place within the collapse—an overlap of 100 percent.

The following three crashes constitute the greatest long-term stock market collapses in modern history.

The Crash of 1937–1938
The Recession of the Great Depression

The crash of 1937–1938 has been called "the Recession of the Great Depression." By early 1937 the American economy had recovered to pre-Depression levels in the areas of production, wages, and profit. But in the spring of 1937 the economy entered a downturn. It continued through much of 1938. It brought the American stock market and economy back to depths not seen since the days of the Great Depression.

Is there any connection between the crash of 1937–1938 and the ancient mystery of the Shemitah? The years 1937 and

1938 just happen to be the same period of time in which falls the Shemitah. The start of the economic downturn came in March 1937 in the Shemitah's approach. The Shemitah's actual commencement day was September 6, 1937. The very day after the Shemitah began, Wall Street collapsed. Starting with this collapse and continuing over the next nine months, America's manufacturing employment fell by a quarter, its industrial output by a third, the stock market by half, and profits by over three quarters. By June of 1937 four million workers lost their jobs.

The stock market's downturn overlapped with the first half of the Shemitah year. Its deep crash began the day after the Shemitah's beginning. The Shemitah overlapped with the financial collapse for six months or 50 percent of its duration, and with the economic collapse for nine months of its duration or 75 percent. The extreme economic plunge took place entirely within the Shemitah's parameters.

The Crash of 2007–2008
The Great Recession

The crash of 2007–2008 is known as the "Great Recession," "the Global Financial Crisis," and "the Second Great Depression." It was the worst financial crisis since the Great Depression. It wiped away trillions of American dollars, threatened the collapse of several major financial institutions, helped trigger the European Sovereign-Debt Crisis, and launched a global recession that would last into 2009. By its end, more than half of the stock market had been wiped out.

Is there any connection with the collapse of 2007–2008 and the ancient mystery? The stock market had been in a continual period of expansion for several years, but less than thirty days from the

Shemitah's commencement in September 2007, the momentum began to change. The stock market began to collapse.

The Shemitah reached its climax one year later in September of 2008. The crash reached its greatest intensity the same month. Its repercussions continued into the spring of the following year. The ancient economic remission and the crash of the Great Recession took place simultaneously. The overlap of the Shemitah to the Great Recession is 100 percent.

The Crash of 1930–1932
The Great Depression

The long-term collapse which began in 1930 and lasted until 1932 would constitute the worst economic and financial crisis in modern history—the core of the Great Depression. Even after the great stock market crashes of 1929, there had been an upward turn. In fact, within six months of the initial crashes, the stock market had returned to early 1929 levels. But in 1930 another downturn began, this time involving a collapse of global trade. Even with this, the market eventually stabilized. But in April of 1931 a downturn began that would bring the world into the depths of the Great Depression. By the end, in July 1932, the amount wiped out of the market was 86 percent. It would take until 1954 for the market to recover its precrash levels.

The years 1930 and 1931 were marked by several key events and developments that would usher in the depths of the Great Depression. In 1930 there would be another stock market collapse as well as the passing of the Smoot-Hawley Tariff Act in mid-June, which would lead to a collapse in global trade and a further descent of the stock market. By late 1930 the world economy began a deep and steady deterioration.

And yet the year 1931 would prove to be even more pivotal. It has been called "the year that made the Great Depression great." In April 1931 a much longer and steadier crash began that brought Wall Street to its lowest levels of the century. The year 1931 was also when a deflationary spiral began, bringing the American and world economies into paralysis.

Could there be any connection between the Great Depression and the ancient mystery? Were it not for what happened during the years 1930 and 1931, the initial recovery could have continued, thus averting "the Great Depression." But it was then that the Shemitah came. The Shemitah took place in 1930–1931.

More specifically, the Shemitah began in late 1930—the same time the world economy began its steady deterioration. In April 1931, the center of the Shemitah year, the stock market began a long-term crash that would bring Wall Street to its lowest levels of the twentieth century and to the depths of the Great Depression.

The seventh year reached its climax with the approach of Tishri, the month that manifests the Shemitah's financial repercussions. On September 19, 1931, an event of seismic proportions took place in the financial world: the British Empire made the decision to discard the gold standard upon which its currency rested. The decision resulted in a worldwide panic that triggered the largest monthly percentage drop in stock market history and plunged the nation and the world into the lowest depths of the Great Depression. When did this global financial cataclysm happen? It took place on the fourteenth day of Tishri, the once-in-seven-year Tishri, the month of the Shemitah's financial repercussions—its climactic autumn wake.

The ancient Shemitah and the Great Depression proceeded simultaneously. The Shemitah fell entirely within and at the core of the Great Depression. Thus the overlap of the Shemitah to the Great Depression is 100 percent.

The Ancient Mystery Behind
the Greatest Collapses of Modern History

We have now looked at the majority of the greatest long-term collapses in stock market history and found an amazing thing: The majority happen according to the timing of the ancient Shemitah. And the connection is not minimal. Rather, the average overlap of the Shemitah to the collapse of the stock market is 85 percent.

If we alter the parameters to include the greatest long-term collapses from the time of the Great Depression onward, the results are just as striking. Of these, over 70 percent of them happen according to the timing of the Shemitah. Of the top five of these crashes, 80 percent of them take place according to the timing of the Shemitah. As for the top two greatest crashes, it becomes 100 percent.

We have opened up the first mystery, a mystery of two realities: the greatest stock market collapses of modern times and an ancient ordinance from Scripture. The two realities would appear worlds apart. How could they possibly be joined in any way? And yet they are bound together, strangely and inexplicably.

————————————

Now we will look at the cycles of the modern financial world, the greatest heights and turning points, and the cycles of the ancient mystery.

Chapter 11

The CYCLES of SINAI

Cycles and Turning Points

THE GREATEST HIGHS or peaks of the stock market constitute turning points—the ending of a period of expansion
and the beginning of decline. A peak in the financial realm,
by definition, will mark the beginning of a downturn or a collapse. A major descent in the stock market will often be connected to an economic collapse, either as its foreshadowing or
its effect.

If the financial and economic realms of ancient Israel could be plotted on a line graph, what would it look like? With the coming of the Shemitah, it would manifest as turning points, very similar to those appearing in a stock market graph. The Sabbath year would, in effect, produce a peak followed by a plummeting line. The descending line would represent the nation's productivity as well as a "remission" in its financial realm.

What happens if we now look at the greatest turning points, the highest apogees in the last forty years of stock market history, along with the key turning points in the economic realm, the recessions and economic downturns of that same period? What will it reveal?

It will certainly include some of the great crashes of modern times, which we have seen in the last chapter—but much more. It will present a progressive record of the financial and economic fortunes of America and the world over the last several peaks and crashes in the order in which they occurred. It will provide a clear and large-scale view of the timing of each turning point as well as the relationship of each turning point to the others.

The data relating to the financial realm will come from the list of the stock market's greatest turning points, its greatest peaks, and troughs of the past forty years. Will any pattern emerge? And is it possible that there will exist any connection to the ancient cycles ordained in the sands of Sinai?

————————————

In the last forty years there have been five major peaks and turning points in stock market history.

First Turning Point: 1973

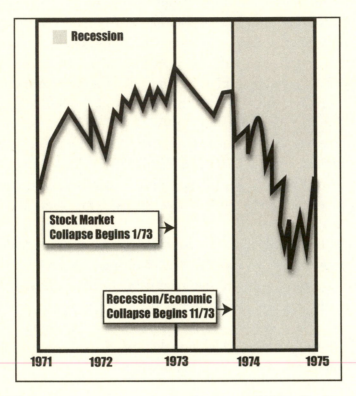

The first turning point comes at the start of 1973. On January 11 the Standard and Poor's (S&P) 500 reached a peak of 120. The market then began a long descent through the rest of the year and through much of the following year. It hit bottom on October 3, 1974, at a level of 62. The loss represented 48 percent of the market's value. The collapse in the financial world foreshadowed and then overlapped with a collapse in the economic realm and a severe global recession.

Second Turning Point: 1980

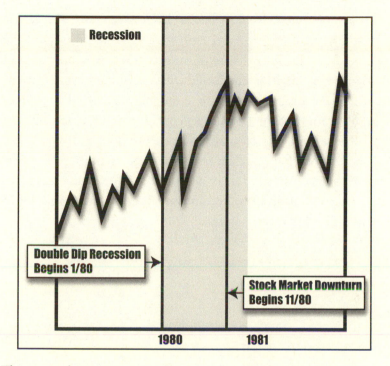

The second turning point happened on November 28, 1980, as the S&P 500 reached a level of 140. After this, came a long descent through all of 1981, reaching its low point on August 12, 1982, at 102, the stock market having lost 27 percent of its value. This collapse had been preceded by an earlier one in 1980, when the Dow Jones Industrial dropped from a level of 903 on February 13 to a low of 759 on April 21.

But the turning point in the financial realm would be preceded by another in the economic realm in January of 1980 as the economy entered a severe recession. This has been thus called a "double-dip recession," and although there would later be a slight recovery, the economy would resume its downward slide in July of 1981. The collapse would affect much of the developed world and witness the highest levels of unemployment since the Great Depression.

The economic crisis had begun even earlier in 1979 as the Iranian Revolution triggered a massive spike in oil prices. The period from 1979 to the beginning of 1980 was one of stagflation, rising inflation combined with declining output growth. During this time the nation's gross national product (GNP) shrank from 5 percent to 1.5 percent. It was 1979 as well that saw the nation's rate of inflation soar into double digits.

So here we have a clustering of turning points. The economic crisis crystalized in 1979, became a worldwide recession in January 1980, and resulted in the fall of the stock market in November of that same year.

Third Turning Point: 1987

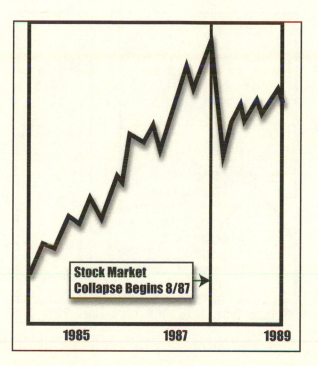

The third turning point came on August 25, 1987. This followed a seven-month boom in stock market prices beginning at the start of the year. At the end of August the S&P 500 reached a peak of 336 and then began to fall. That collapse contained, in October, the greatest stock market percentage crash in American history, known as "Black Monday."

The descent was short lived, reaching its conclusion on December 4, 1987, at a low point of 224. Its short and unique nature avoided triggering a recession. But in its brief duration its impact was severe, causing the market to lose over 33 percent of its worth. It took two years to regain the levels lost in August 1987. It became one of the most enigmatic collapses in financial history. Its causes are still debated to this day.

Fourth Turning Point: 2000

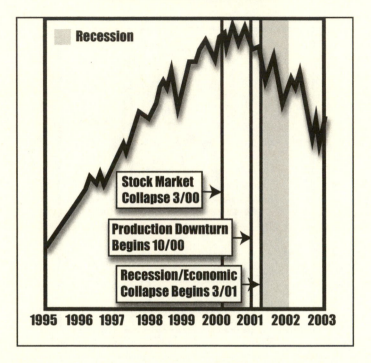

The stock market reached its fourth major apogee on March 24, 2000, attaining a level of 1,527. Its fall coincided with the bursting of the Dot-Com Bubble. This led to an economic recession in March of 2001. The recession continued until November of 2001. In the midst of the recession came 9/11. The impact of the events of 9/11 caused one of the most dramatic collapses in Wall Street history and further crippled the nation's financial realm. The market continued a long descent until hitting bottom on October 9, 2002, having lost 49 percent of its value. In this case the financial collapse preceded, exceeded, and contained the economic collapse.

Fifth Turning Point: 2007

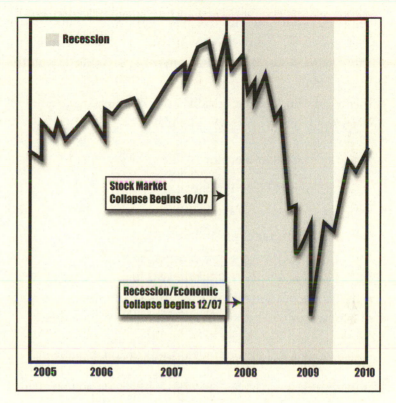

The fifth turning point took place on October 9, 2007, when the S&P 500 peaked at 1,565. The stock market then began a dramatic year-and-a-half collapse. Soon after the financial turning point came the economic turning point as the economy entered into recession in December 2007. The financial collapse reached its lowest point on March 9, 2009, at 676, having lost over 56 percent of its value. Three months later, in June 2009, the recession drew to its close. The period between apogee and the trough became known as "the Great Recession."

The Mystery of Cycles

We have just looked at the five major peaks in modern stock market history or the five major turning points and collapses in the financial world. Is there anything striking about the resulting picture?

When do the greatest peaks and key turning points of modern stock market history take place?

- The first takes place in 1973.
- The second takes place in 1980.
- The third takes place in 1987.
- The fourth takes place in 2000.
- And the fifth takes place in 2007.

What is the relationship of one peak to the next? The math is, of course, simple, but for the sake of clarity, here it is:

- The first and second peaks and turning points, of 1973 and 1980—a cycle of seven years
- The second and third peaks, of 1980 and 1987—a cycle of seven years
- The fourth and fifth peaks, of 2000 and 2007—a cycle of seven years

The mystery of the Shemitah ordains that an economic and financial transformation take place in the seventh year. Thus these two realms are altered according to a seven-year cycle. What we see now in the rise and fall of the stock market is that all five of the greatest peaks or turning points in modern financial history are connected to the preceding peak or the following peak by a cycle of seven years.

Crashes of 1973, 1980, and 1987
Seven-Year Cycles

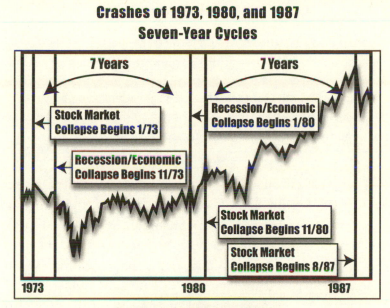

Crashes of 2000 and 2007
Seven-Year Cycle

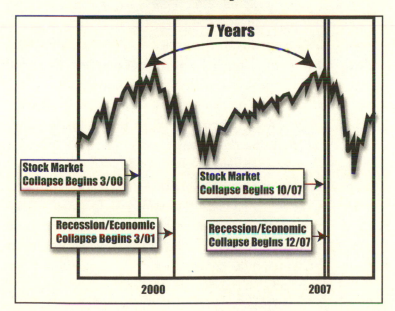

The Crash Cycles

According to the ancient mystery, in the seventh year there is to occur a cessation in the nation's economic and financial realms.

> In the seventh year there shall be a sabbath of solemn rest for the land, a sabbath to the LORD. You shall neither sow your field nor prune your vineyard.
> —LEVITICUS 25:4

If we go back to our theoretical graph charting ancient Israel's Year of the Shemitah, we would find peaking and plunging lines. The lines charting Israel's Shemitah in economic turns would represent an economic downturn or recession. The lines charting the Shemitah on a financial graph would represent a financial collapse. If we now take this into the modern world and look at the graphs representing the American and global economic and financial realms, what do we find? We find the same phenomenon. The one line represents financial collapse and the other represents economic recession.

If we go back again to our theoretical graph of ancient Israel and expand it to cover a period of several decades, what will we find? We find that the Shemitah years have produced several of these peaking and plunging lines more or less evenly distributed throughout the time covered in the graph. More specifically we find that these peaks and slopes are connected to the other peaks and slopes by a cycle of seven years.

What happens if we now do the same thing with our graphs covering the actual financial and economic fortunes of the modern world of the last four decades? We find the same ancient phenomenon reappears. The greatest peaks and downturns are distributed more or less evenly over the period. More specifically, we find that the five greatest peaks and crashes are connected to the preceding or succeeding peaks and down-turns by a cycle of seven years.

The Sacred Cycles
and the Five Collapses

We have witnessed an amazing correlation. In the past four decades of modern history the economic and financial realms of America and the world have followed the ancient mystery that ordains economic cessation and financial collapse *taking place according to a seven-year cycle.*

But could there be more to the mystery? Is it possible that any of these collapses could be joined to the Shemitah in a still more specific way? The Shemitah is based not just on a seven-year cycle but on a *specific* seven-year cycle ordained in the Bible. Only *one out of seven years* can be the actual appointed Year of the Shem-itah. Could any of the five great peaks, apogees, downturns, and collapses of the last four decades bear a more specific connection to the *once-in-seven-years* Shemitah of ancient times?

The Test: We will now take one more look at the five peaks and the five collapses of modern times. But this time we will have one specific focus—that of timing. Do any of these peaks and collapses bear any connection to the timing ordained in the ancient mystery?

The Mystery of
the First Turning Point

The sequence begins in the winter of 1973, January 11, when the S&P 500 reached its peak of 120 and then began a long descent. The first Shemitah of this period began in September

1972 and continued to September 1973. Four months after the Shemitah began, the stock market collapsed. Thus the peak and the crash took place entirely within the biblical Shemitah

The First Collapse and the Biblical Shemitah

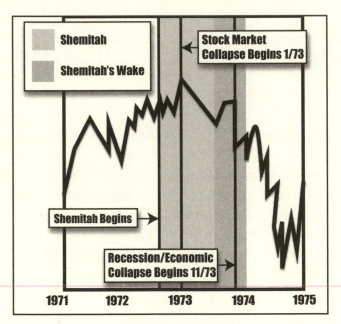

The financial collapse then coincided with a global economic recession. The recession began in the Shemitah's wake, autumn 1973.

The Mystery of
the Second Turning Point

Seven years later the American economy fell into a recession that constituted one of the most severe downturns of modern times. The first phase of a double-dip economic collapse began in January 1980. Is there any connection between this and the ancient mystery?

Again, the answer is yes. The Shemitah began in 1979—the same year that the economic crisis began—a year that saw a dramatic surge of inflation, an energy crisis, and a steady decline of growth output. Four months after the Shemitah began, the economy began its descent.

The Second Collapse and the Biblical Shemitah

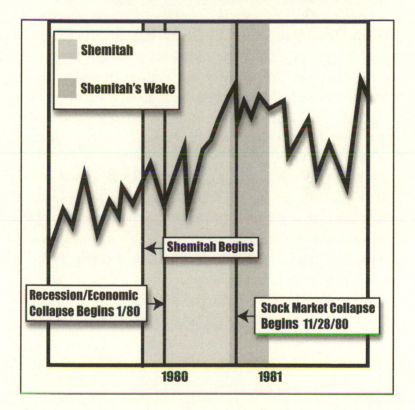

Thus the recession of 1980 began in the midst of the Shemitah. The financial realm followed with a collapse beginning in the Shemitah's wake, the autumn of 1980.

The Mystery of
the Third Turning Point

Seven years later the stock market reached its next apogee as the S&P 500 peaked at 336 on August 25, 1987. It then began its collapse, a collapse that involved the greatest single-day percentage crash in Wall Street history. Is there any connection between these events and the ancient mystery?

The answer is, again, yes. From the end of the recession in the early 1980s onward the American economy had been in a phase of rapid expansion. But in the latter part of 1986 came the third Shemitah of the forty-year period. That same year a shift took place. In 1986 the period of rapid economic growth came to an end and was replaced by an economic slowdown. The Shemitah then coincided with most of 1987, ending in September of that year.

Only one month of Elul in seven years can complete the Shemitah and begin the buildup to the end of the seven-year cycle. The Elul of the seventh year began on August 26, 1987. That same day the stock market changed its momentum and began to collapse. As the Hebrew month progressed, the stock market grew increasingly unstable.

On October 19, 1987, came the greatest stock market percentage crash in Wall Street history—Black Monday.

The Third Collapse and the Biblical Shemitah

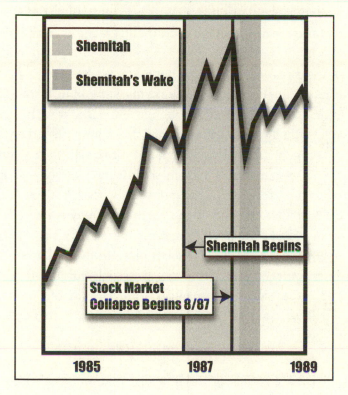

The crash took place in the one month of Tishri in seven years that begins at the Shemitah's moment of financial nullification and manifests its repercussions.

The Other Collapse

Even though the 1990s did not see a significant stock market collapse, a massive implosion nevertheless did take place in the financial realm. The stock market is only one component of the financial market—the other is the bond market. The bond market is actually the greater of the two, typically twice the size of the stock market.

Though the bond market is traditionally considered to be safer and less volatile than the stock market, the 1990s saw one of the greatest and most dramatic collapses in the history of the bond market. So great and dramatic was the collapse that it was named "The Great Bond Market Massacre." *Fortune* magazine called it the worst bond market loss in history.[1] It is said that those who lived through it remember it with "horror."

When did it happen? It happened in the year 1994, the year of the Shemitah. The collapse began in February, in the Shemitah's center. It began with a sudden sell off in America and Japan, which then spread across the industrial world. Between January and September, the end of the Shemitah, the yield on US long-term bonds mushroomed over one hundred fifty basis points.[2]

Again the year of the Shemitah brought in a collapse. Again the phenomenon had struck the financial realm. This time it was the other side of the financial world, causing the loss of over $1.5 trillion in assets, wiping out $1.5 billion of actual debt.[3]

The Other Turning Point

As for the other side of the financial realm, the stock market, even here a striking change takes place.

Once a Shemitah and its most overt consequences are over, the next phase, that of buildup or recovery, can begin. If one looks at a stock market chart of the 1990s, one will notice a striking change. In view of what would come next, the growth at the beginning of the decade appears mild, if not strained. But then appears a noticeable turning point.

The Other Turning Point and the Post-Shemitah Boom

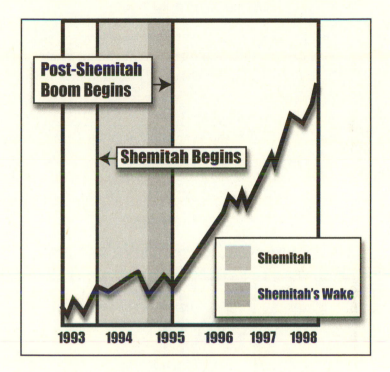

The stock market suddenly begins to turn markedly upward. The expansion is dramatic and remarkable. It will continue until the time of the next crash.

The Shemitah ends in the autumn of 1994. The sudden upward turn begins at the start of 1995—right at the end of the Shemitah's wake. Thus the resulting stock market boom of the late 1990s began at the end of the Shemitah of 1994 and would come to an end with the approach of the following Shemitah.

The Mystery of
the Fourth Turning Point

In the year 2000 the stock market boom reached its peak and began a long descent that would last over two and a half years. In March 2001 the economy changed direction and fell into recession. In September came the attack of 9/11, which paralyzed the world's financial markets.

The year 2000 is also the year the Shemitah began. As it did, the stock market was in descent, and the recession, in the spring of 2001, commenced at its center point. In the middle of that Shemitah year the two collapses combined. The convergence concluded in the Shemitah's autumn wake.

The Fourth Collapse and the Biblical Shemitah

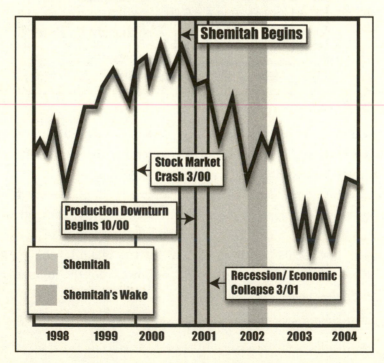

The Shemitah ended on September 17, 2001. It would thus contain the calamity of 9/11 and its traumatic impact on the American and global financial realms.

The Mystery of the Fifth Turning Point

The stock market reached its next peak on October 9, 2007, then turned downward in what would become one of the greatest collapses in stock market history. In December of 2007 the economy descended into recession. The financial collapse lasted until March 2009, while the economic recession ended three months later. Is there any connection to these events and the mystery of the Shemitah?

The next Shemitah of this period began in September 2007. With its coming the world's financial markets began to turn. In fact, it was in the Shemitah's opening month that the stock market's years of ascending ended and the collapse began. And three months after the Shemitah's starting point the economy began to collapse as well.

The Fifth Collapse and the Biblical Shemitah

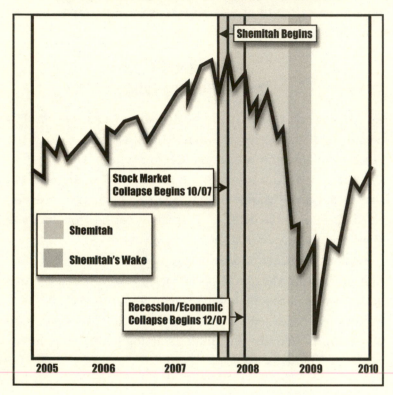

Both collapses took place on historic scales. Both began in the Year of the Shemitah. And before that Shemitah was over, it would bring the greatest point crash in stock market history. The majority of what we today call the "Great Recession" was actually the Year of the Shemitah.

The Sinai Cycles

We have found an amazing phenomenon:

1. In the Bible the economic and financial realms are timed to a seven-year cycle. This cycle concerns

an economic cessation and a financial remission centering on the seventh year in the cycle.

2. Behind the past four decades of financial and economic history is a seven-year cycle. This cycle concerns the greatest financial collapses and crashes together with economic downturns and recessions. The record reveals an amazing phenomenon: all the greatest peaks and crashes of the past forty years take place in a seven-year cycle with regard to the previous or subsequent collapse.

3. The greatest peaks and collapses of the past forty years are not just timed to a seven-year cycle but to a *specific* seven-year cycle. They are timed specifically to the ancient biblical year of economic cessation and financial remission—the Shemitah. In other words, behind the great crashes and economic recessions of modern times lies the ancient mystery of the Shemitah.

In other time periods this pattern does not necessarily appear as obvious, consistent, or present as it does here. The reason that the period beginning with 1973 may be especially significant will be addressed in a later chapter.

The facts remain, and they all point to the ancient mystery. Here are some of them:

- The greatest financial turning points of the past forty years have been connected to the Shemitah or its wake *100 percent of the time!*

- The greatest financial turning points, peaks, or long-term collapses of the past forty years that have taken place within the biblical Year of the Shemitah or its autumn wake is *100 percent!*

- Where there has been both a financial collapse and an economic recession, the period connecting their starting points has fallen within the biblical Shemitah *100 percent of the time!*

- Thus, from the forty-year period beginning in 1973, every single one of the five greatest financial and economic peaks and collapses have converged, clustered, and taken place according to the set time of the Shemitah.

We have looked into the greatest overall collapses and crashes in modern American and world history and found within them a three-thousand-year-old mystery determining their course.

But what if we embark on a different quest? What if, rather than looking at the greatest turning points and overall long-term collapses, we look instead at the greatest *single-day* crashes in stock market history? These are governed by different laws. What will we find?

The results will be no less amazing.

Chapter 12

The MYSTERY of CATACLYSMS

The Days of Collapse

Up to now our search has focused on the *long-term* crashes of the financial and economic world, collapses spread out over a period of months and generally lasting more than a year's time. But now we begin a new search. We will now look at the stock market's greatest *one-day crashes*.

The search is different and will involve different principles and dynamics. Long-term collapses tend, by nature, to be caused or affected by long-term conditions, trends, and dynamics. But single-day crashes are more volatile, unpredictable, and susceptible to fluke circumstances and "chance" factors. A good example of this is the Black Monday crash of 1987, the causes of which have been attributed to everything from rising interest rates to the quirks of computer trading programs.

The Shemitah's Other Keys

Another major difference between long-term crashes and single-day crashes is, of course, the time frame. A long-term collapse will generally involve several seasons. A single-day crash will, by definition, involve a single season, month, and date. So beyond the component of the seventh year, we will now be able to look deeper at the Shemitah's other components—namely the *time of year, the month, and the days.* We will now more clearly be able to see if there exists any connection between modern financial collapses and...

- *Elul,* the month that leads in and builds up to the Shemitah's beginning and its climactic conclusion.

- *Tishri,* the month most central to the Shemitah, that which marks the seventh year at its beginning and manifests its financial repercussions at its end.

- *The Shemitah's wake,* the season that immediately follows the Shemitah's Day of Remission and manifests its repercussions.

Having now the keys, let us begin the search.

The Ten Greatest Single-Day Point
Crashes in Stock Market History

For our first search we will look at the ten greatest *point* crashes in Wall Street history. These are the financial collapses in which the greatest number of stock market points were wiped away.

The Seven-Year Key and
the Ten Greatest Point Crashes

Of the ten greatest stock market point crashes in history, are any of them connected to the Year of the Shemitah? Since the Year of the Shemitah comes around only once in seven years, the chances would be one in seven. There are ten crashes on the list. So the chances of any one of these crashes taking place in the Year of the Shemitah is 15 percent. But if there was something else going on, then the number would be greater than 15 percent.

Do any of these crashes have a connection to the Year of the Shemitah? The answer is yes. Is the percentage greater than 15 percent? The answer is, again, yes. How many of the greatest single-day point crashes in Wall Street history are connected to the Year of the Shemitah?

The majority of them!

Over half of the greatest point crashes in Wall Street history are joined to the biblical Year of Remission. An incredible *60 percent* of the ten greatest crashes take place either within the Shemitah or in its wake. Or to put it another way, only a *minority* of the greatest crashes take place *outside* the biblical Year of the Shemitah.

The Tishri Key and the
Greatest Point Crashes

Now let's take another component of the ancient mystery and see if it bears any relation to the greatest crashes in Wall Street history. Are any of these greatest point crashes linked to the Shemitah's key month of Tishri, including the day on which Tishri begins at sunset?

There are twelve months in the Hebrew year, with the exception of a thirteenth "leap month" inserted in the calendar about every three years. So the odds that any of the ten greatest stock market crashes would take place in the Hebrew month of Tishri are a little less than one in twelve. Thus we could expect that, at best, one of the ten greatest point crashes might fall in Tishri—or none at all. But if something more than natural were going on, then the number would be greater than one in ten.

So do any of these crashes have a connection to the Hebrew month of Tishri? The answer is yes.

How many of the greatest single-day point crashes in stock market history are connected to the Hebrew month of Tishri? *The majority of them!*

Over half of the greatest stock market crashes in Wall Street history are connected to this single solitary Hebrew month. The number is *60 percent*. That the majority of the crashes should cluster around a single Hebrew month—and that only *a minority* take place outside of it—is remarkable.

The Last Tishri and
the Greatest Point Crashes

Do any of the greatest financial collapses that fall in the month of Tishri fall specifically on the *Tishri of the seventh year*—and, even more specifically, do any of them fall on the critical Tishri that *closes* the seventh year?

The answer is: 80 percent of them!

More than at any other time of the year, and more than any other time in seven years, they fall on the Tishri that closes the Shemitah. The majority of the greatest point crashes in history just happen to take place in a very small period of time that comes around once in seven years, which also just happens to be the same time on the biblical calendar for manifesting the massive financial repercussions of the seventh year.

Connecting the Puzzle Pieces

The seventh year, the month of Tishri, and, specifically, the Tishri that appears at the close of the seventh year are all components of the mystery. As signs they may appear independent of the others—one in one crash, another in another. But what happens if we put it all together, taking the greatest point crashes in modern stock market history and holding them up against the components of the ancient mystery?

How many of the ten greatest point crashes in Wall Street history are connected either to the biblical month of Tishri or the biblical Year of the Shemitah? *70 percent!*

How many of the ten greatest point crashes in Wall Street history are connected either to the biblical month of Tishri or the biblical Year of the Shemitah, including the Shemitah's lead-in months? *80 percent!*

The Autumn Phenomenon
and the Ancient Mystery

The strange clustering of financial collapses in the autumn—particularly in the month of September/October—has mystified financial analysts for years. In earlier times some sought to explain the phenomenon by linking it to the depletion of cash reserves caused by farmers getting paid for their autumn harvests. But this and other attempted explanations have all failed as times and conditions have changed, as have the factors behind the stock market crashes of modern times. It has remained a mysterious and inexplicable phenomenon. And yet the amazing thing is that while financial analysts have noted this strange phenomenon of stock market collapses gravitating to the autumn and have found it inexplicable, the very same time is appointed by God in Scripture for financial nullification.

The mystery of the Shemitah provides the missing keys. It reveals the ancient biblical connection joining together the autumn with the financial implosion. The key is not simply the season of autumn or the month of October, but specifically the biblical month of Tishri and its lead-in month of Elul. Added to this is the second key—that of the seven-year cycle and, *specifically*, the *specific seven-year cycle* of the Shemitah. When you then hold up the financial collapses of modern history to the ancient mystery, the revelation becomes amazingly clear.

The Other Cataclysms

If the ancient mystery is at work, we should expect it to leave its fingerprints in more than one sphere of financial cataclysm. We now move into the second of the two major spheres of collapses—the percentage crashes.

The greatest point crashes in stock market history are those in which the greatest volume or market points are wiped away. But there is another measure and category of financial collapse— the greatest *percentage crashes*. In these it is not the *volume* or *magnitude* of the crash that counts, but how much was wiped away in proportion to the overall market—the percentage lost. The greatest percentage crashes in Wall Street history take place over a wide span of time—from 1899–2008. Do these crashes of percentage reveal anything beyond the natural?

The Eighteen Days of Tishri

Of the ten greatest percentage crashes in stock market history, do any of them take place in the biblical month of Tishri? We start out again with a one-in-twelve chance for any event to take place in this single month. And, again, we have only ten crashes. So we might expect perhaps *one* of the ten greatest percentage crashes to have happened in that Hebrew month—or *none*. What is the answer?

Forty percent of the greatest percentage crashes in Wall Street history take place in this single Hebrew month. No other month comes close.

If we enlarge our search by just three days, how many of the ten greatest percentage crashes take place in the month of Tishri or within three days of Tishri? *Sixty percent!*

How big is the span of time in which all these stock market crashes cluster? *Just eighteen days!*

Thus *60 percent* of the greatest single-day percentage crashes in Wall Street history cluster around a tiny sliver of the biblical year. They all take place within the same eighteen biblical days.

If there was nothing more than the natural at work, the greatest crashes should be distributed randomly, more or less evenly, throughout every month and season of the year. But for 60 percent of these crashes to cluster around one time period of the year, and one small time period, points to something more than natural going on.

The Ten Greatest Stock Market
Percentage Crashes (in Hebrew)

Month	Crashes
NISAN	
IYYAR	
SIVAN	
TAMMUZ	10
AV	6
ELUL	
TISHRI	1 2 3 9
HESHVAN	4 8
KISLEV	
TEVET	5
SHEVAT	
ADAR	7

A span of eighteen days represents less than 5 percent of the year. The chances of any one of these crashes to take place during this short space of time would be 5 percent. But instead of 5 percent, we have the *majority* of them doing that—or 60 percent of the greatest stock market crashes all occurring in a span of time representing 5 percent of the year! And this 5 percent of the year happens to fall in the critical month of Tishri. Only a minority of the great crashes take place outside this very tiny fraction of days.

The Mystery Behind the
Greatest Postwar Percentage Crashes

What if we update our search field to the percentage crashes in the post–World War II era?

- From the top eight greatest postwar percentage crashes, do any of them take place in the biblical month of financial repercussions, in Tishri or its eve? *The majority—62.5 percent!*

- Are any of these crashes connected to the Shemitah or its climactic wake? *Yes, 87.5 percent!*

- How many of these crashes are either connected to the Shemitah, its wake, or the biblical month of Tishri? *One hundred percent!*

The Mystery Behind the
Twenty Greatest Percentage Crashes

What if we now expand the search beyond the top ten to the top twenty greatest single-day percentage crashes? Will the connection to the mystery of the Shemitah still hold?

Of the twenty greatest percentage crashes in Wall Street history, how many are linked to the month of Tishri? *Forty-five percent of them are linked to the month of Tishri.*

How many of them are linked to the Year of the Shemitah? *Fifty percent of them!*

How many are linked to the month of Tishri, its eve, the Shemitah, or its wake? *Seventy-five percent of them!*

The connection to the mystery holds and consistently so.

The Ancient Mystery and the
Twenty Greatest Point Crashes

What if we now do the same thing with the greatest *point* crashes in stock market history, expanding the search beyond the top ten to the top twenty? Will the connection to the mystery of the Shemitah still hold?

Of the top twenty point crashes in stock market history, how many are linked to the Elul-Tishri cycle? *Over half of them—55 percent!*

How many of the crashes are specifically linked to the climactic end of the Shemitah, the time of financial remission? *Seventy percent of them!*

How many crashes are connected to the Year of the Shemitah? *Seventy-five percent of them!*

How many are linked to the month of Elul, its eve, the Year of the Shemitah, or its wake? *Eighty-five percent of them!*

The phenomenon again manifests, strangely, consistently, and amazingly so.

The Mystery of Proximity

What happens if we take the five greatest point crashes in stock market history and see how close each falls to the Shemitah's greatest point of impact concerning the financial realm—the point where Elul and Tishri converge at the end of the Shemitah year? Since the point of impact can only affect that which comes after it (and not before), we will mark the crash by where it falls within the seven-year period, how near or far it occurs from the Shemitah's point of greatest impact. If nothing more than natural is at work, we would expect the crashes to average out to a proximity of about 50 percent, or to fall on average about three and a half years away from the Shemitah's end, the halfway mark in the seven-year cycle. But what we find is dramatically different and amazing.

The Fifth Greatest Stock Market Point Crash
Proximity to Biblical Point of Impact—99.609 percent!

The Fourth Greatest Stock Market Point Crash
Proximity to Biblical Point of Impact—97.54 percent!

The Third Greatest Stock Market Point Crash
Proximity to Biblical Point of Impact—100 percent!

The Second Greatest Stock Market Point Crash
Proximity to Biblical Point of Impact—99.375 percent!

The First Greatest Stock Market Point Crash
Proximity to Biblical Point of Impact—100 percent!

Average proximity and convergence of the five greatest stock market point crashes to the Shemitah's point of greatest impact: *99.305 percent!*

The Mystery Behind the Top Five
Greatest Postwar Percentage Crashes

Of the top five greatest percentage crashes of the postwar era, how many of them took place either in the wake of the Shemitah's climax or at the moment of climax itself? *One hundred percent!*

The Mystery Behind the Top Five
Greatest Point Crashes in History

Of the five greatest point crashes in American history, how many of them took place either in the wake of the Shemitah's climax or at the moment of climax itself? *One hundred percent!*

The Three Greatest Percentage Crashes
and Three Hebrew Days

The top three greatest percentage crashes in Wall Street history bear either the name "Black Monday" or "Black Tuesday." Do they bear any connection to the mystery of the Shemitah, which determines Tishri as the key month of financial repercussions? Here are the three greatest percentage crashes in history revealing their dates on the biblical calendar:

The Second Greatest Percentage Crash: Black Monday 1929
Tishri 24

The Third Greatest Percentage Crash: Black Tuesday 1929
Tishri 25

The First Greatest Percentage Crash: Black Monday 1987
Tishri 26

Thus of the three greatest percentage crashes in Wall Street history, and of all the days in the calendar on which they could take place—they all happen within a span of *three days* on the biblical calendar.

The Greatest of All Crashes

What if we just looked at the two greatest crashes of all time—the greatest point crash in history and the greatest percentage crash in history? What would it reveal?

Each crash is connected to the month of Tishri. One takes place in the midst of Tishri and the other on the day that begins it.

Each takes place at the end of the seven-year biblical cycle, the Shemitah's climactic conclusion or wake—the time ordained in the ancient mystery for massive transformations and remission in the financial realm and for the manifesting of its repercussions.

———————

We have lifted up this measuring rod: if there was nothing more than the natural at work in the greatest collapses in history, then the greatest financial collapses in history should be more or less evenly distributed throughout the year. We have searched the matter on several grounds and applied several probes, tests, and parameters.

The conclusion: Something very much more than natural is indeed going on. And the signs of the phenomenon all point to the same ancient biblical mystery. If the collapse of the world's stock markets were an act of crime, the Shemitah would have long ago been indicted for the evidence left at the crime scene. In its numbers, its connections, its convergences, its per-centages, its magnitude, and its consistency, the amount of fingerprints covering the financial cataclysms of modern times is overwhelming.

––––––––––––––

We now take the mystery to another level. The mystery of the Shemitah is not only a phenomenon operating behind the world's economic and financial realms—it is also a phenomenon linked to judgment. Is it possible that the dynamics of the Shemitah are moving increasingly toward judgment? The answer will lie with the transpiring of a calamitous event and the days in which the mystery of Shemitah coalesces with the mystery of the harbingers.

PART IV

THE MYSTERY OF THE SHEMITAH AND THE DAYS OF THE HARBINGERS

Chapter 13

The 9/11 SHEMITAH

The Days of Harbingers

THE MYSTERY THAT begins in the wilderness of Sinai has a larger context—judgment. The Shemitah can bring blessing or judgment. To a nation that has turned against the God of its foundation and driven Him out of its life, the Shemitah comes as a sign of judgment that specifically strikes that nation's source of blessings and sustenance, its financial and economic realms.

Is it possible that if such a national apostasy grows more marked and severe, that the signs of the Shemitah will likewise grow more marked and severe accordingly? And is it possible that we are already witnessing this phenomenon?

We now move to another stage in which the mystery of the Shemitah will combine with the mystery of the harbingers. It will do so in the form of a calamity of national and global proportions.

The Shemitah Begins

It is the year 2000. The American economy has been undergoing an extended period of economic expansion, the longest on record. At the same time America's departure from God has been continuous and progressive. A Shemitah is coming. In the spring preceding the Shemitah, the stock market begins to decline. Its fall will continue into 2002.

The Shemitah begins September 2000. Though the stock market is descending, the economic realm is not yet in recession. Several factors are taken into account in declaring the start of a recession. One of these is employment, another is sales, and another is production.

In March 2001 employment reaches a peak and begins to decline. This, combined with other economic signs of decline, will constitute the beginning of a recession. So in the spring of 2001, the center of the Shemitah, both the stock market and the economy, the nation's financial and economic realms, are collapsing together.

And yet, one of the key factors of a recession is industrial production. Several months before the recession was declared, America's industrial production began to decline. Within a year the decline reached 6 percent, surpassing the production declines of past recessions.

When did the downturn begin? America's industrial production peaked in September of 2000 and then began to decline. The Shemitah, by definition, causes production to decline. When did the Shemitah begin? The Shemitah's exact beginning was September 30, 2000. When did the decline in production begin? At September's end. The Shemitah of 2001 and the downturn of the nation's industrial production began simultaneously.

The Shemitah's Climax:
September 2001

The Shemitah, as we have seen, begins almost unnoticeably, as to outward appearance, but then builds in intensity as it heads towards its dramatic and climactic conclusion on Elul 29, the Day of Remission.

The Shemitah began in the autumn of 2000. The first signs of economic downturn followed. By the spring the economy had descended into recession. But it was as the Shemitah headed to the autumn of 2001 that its dramatic climax took place.

First Warning

What are the signs of a nation in danger of judgment? One of the classic biblical signs of national judgment is this: Years before the destruction falls, a warning is given. The nation's hedge of protection is removed. Its borders and national security are breached. An enemy is allowed to make a strike into the land. The strike is contained, limited in time and scope. It is a shaking, a wake-up call, an alarm—the first massive warning of judgment. The nation is then given a grace period to either turn back to God or to continue on its course and head to destruction—the first harbinger.

The first harbinger was manifested on American soil on September 11, 2001, as America's hedge of protection was lifted. An enemy was allowed to make an incursion, a strike on the land. America's national security was breached. The strike was contained, limited in time and scope. It was a shaking, a wake-up call, an alarm. But in the wake of 9/11 America did exactly as ancient Israel did in the wake of the ancient attack. America refused to turn back and, in fact, became even more defiant in its apostasy. And the ancient harbingers of judgment then began to manifest.

But 9/11 didn't take place in just any year; *9/11 took place in the Year of the Shemitah.*

The Shemitah of 9/11

As the Shemitah especially impacts the nation's financial and economic realms, so too did 9/11. The calamity struck lower Manhattan, also known as the "financial district." The twin towers stood as symbols of America's economic and financial preeminence. The calamity struck the heart of America's financial sector as it created a shock wave that opened a crack in one of Wall Street's most famous buildings.

But 9/11 struck Wall Street in a more direct way—it paralyzed it. It forced the New York Stock Exchange to close down. The calamity took place on Tuesday. Its impact forced Wall Street to shut down for almost a week. The following Monday was set for the reopening of the stock market. It was September 17, 2001. Wall Street collapsed. The market plunged 684 points in one session. It was the greatest stock market point crash in American history up to that day.

So here we have yet another one of the great stock market crashes in world history. And here, again, the ancient mystery of the Shemitah manifests:

- The crash of 2001 is linked to the Year of the Shemitah.

- It takes place in September 2001, the time of the Shemitah's climactic end.

- It is joined to the biblical month of Tishri, the time of financial repercussions. On the very night of the crash Tishri will begin.

- It constitutes a mass nullification of the financial realm "at the end of the seventh year," the time ordained in the Bible for mass nullification of the financial realm.

Elul 29, 2001

But there's more. The mystery of the Shemitah centers on one day above every other—the Day of Nullification, the very last and climactic day, Elul 29, the day when financial accounts are wiped away. When did the greatest financial crash in American history up to that day take place?

The greatest financial crash in American history up to that day took place on Elul 29, the biblical Day of the Shemitah.

The greatest financial collapse in American history up to that day took place on the very day given in the Bible to wipe away the financial accounts of a nation. It not only fell on Elul 29, but it also fell on the one Elul 29 that comes around only once in seven years and is appointed to cause mass nullification in a nation's financial realm.

2001: Elul 29—Biblical Day of Financial Collapse

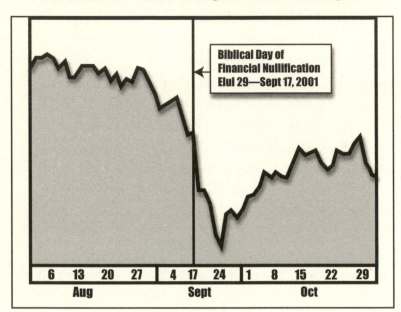

Biblical Day of
Financial Nullification
Elul 29—Sept 17, 2001

| 6 | 13 | 20 | 27 | 4 | 17 | 24 | 1 | 8 | 15 | 22 | 29 |

Aug   Sept   Oct

The Elul 29 Sunset

It happened on the exact day, down to the exact hours. The ancient command ordains that financial accounts be wiped clean "at the end of the seventh year." The end of the seventh year, as we have seen, was taken to mean the last day of the seventh year, Elul 29, and, more specifically, the end of that day, sunset. Thus all accounts of debt and credit had to be wiped clean and nullified by the time the sun went down on Elul 29. At the moment of sunset they were reckoned as nullified.

So Elul 29 was the day of canceling one's debts, one's credits, and nullifying financial accounts before sunset. But at the moment of sunset it was Tishri. Beyond that, it was a holy day when the trumpets are sounded. So in the hours leading to sunset, Jewish people would prepare for the high holy days. The remission of Elul 29 had to be completed by late afternoon.

The Day of Nullification

So on Elul 29, 2001, the Day of Nullification, came the greatest nullification, cancellation, and wiping away of financial accounts in the nation's history up to that day—the most massive single-day transformation of America's financial realm ever recorded. That day, around the world, observant Jews were symbolically nullifying their accounts while on Wall Street accounts were being nullified in reality. It was the Shemitah sweeping through the New York Stock Exchange. It was Wall Street's most colossal nullification—and it was all taking place on the ancient Day of the Shemitah.

And then, just a few hours before sunset, in late afternoon, it was over. The Day of the Shemitah was finished, the Year of the Shemitah was complete, and the seven-year cycle had come to a close. The greatest financial collapse in Wall Street history was also finished, just in time for the sunset closing of the seventh year.

The final days of the Shemitah are its most intense and dramatic of days. So too the final days of the Shemitah 2001 were its most intense and dramatic of days. And 9/11 was part of it. It would mark the Shemitah's final week and complete a cycle that had begun seven years earlier.

And there was another connection between 9/11 and the end of the seventh year. Since 9/11 had caused Wall Street to shut down for almost a week, it meant that the stock market had been, in effect, frozen in time as it approached its reopening on Elul 29. In other words, the Day of Remission opened up on the number appointed for 9/11. Or in other words, the number that appeared the morning of Elul 29 and from which the collapse of Wall Street began was the same number that appeared the morning of 9/11 when the calamity began. As far as the stock market was concerned, there was no space between the two days. September 11 and Elul 29 were joined together. The opening of the one became the opening of the other. The same number would again appear on Wall Street eight years later—*on the same day*—the anniversary of 9/11. Investors were reportedly "spooked" by the occurrence.

9/11 and the Ancient Mystery

The link between 9/11 and Elul 29 raises an inescapable point: Had the events of 9/11 not happened, there would have been no collapse of the stock market. And if the attack had not happened at the time it happened, then the stock market would not have collapsed at the time it did. And if the stock market hadn't collapsed at the time it did, there would have been no great financial collapse in the Year of the Shemitah. Nor would there have been any transformation of the financial realm. Nor would there have been a connection between Wall Street and Tishri. Nor would the mass nullification of the nation's financial accounts have taken place on the exact day appointed from ancient times for the wiping away of a nation's financial accounts. It couldn't have taken place in a more precise way. Without the calamity of 9/11 happening when it did, the ancient mystery of the Shemitah could not have been fulfilled as it was fulfilled on the exact day at "the end of seven years"—Elul 29.

What this means is that even the timing of 9/11 had to be part of the ancient mystery of the Shemitah. If that sounds like a radical proposition, remember 586 BC when the armies of Babylon brought destruction to the land of Israel. And yet the secret of its timing was tied to the mystery of the Shemitah—so too with what took place in September 2001, the timing was tied to the ancient mystery.

The Global Mystery

What does it reveal? It reveals that the mystery of the Shemitah touches every realm of life, involves the entire world, and alters the course of history. It is not of natural origin or explanation—but supernatural. In view of this, let's look again at the description of the Shemitah in its greatest and most far-reaching manifestation:

- It operates on an epic and global scale, transcending national borders and involving every realm of life.

- It involves the political realm, the cultural realm, the sociological realm, the military realm, and even the natural realm.

- Though it directly impacts the financial and economic realms, its outworking can be triggered and accompanied by events of entirely different realms.

- It can manifest in the form of a cataclysmic event.

- It can wipe away not only financial accounts but also physical realities, buildings, walls, towers, and cities.

- It can alter the landscape of nations and powers.

The Shemitah's manifestation in September 2001 was astonishingly precise, stunning, and world-changing. But it would be followed by yet another manifestation of the ancient mystery, equally precise, equally stunning, and equally world-changing.

Chapter 14

The SHEMITAH and the GREAT RECESSION

The Second Shaking

THE MYSTERY OF *The Harbinger* reveals an ancient template of national judgment now replaying in modern America. This template reveals a specific progression from the moment of the nation's first shaking in the form of an enemy strike, to the day of its destruction. Two of the keys involved in this progression are these:

1. If the nation rejects the first shaking and warning of judgment, there will come another, and another, until the nation either returns to God or descends into the full end of judgment.

2. "The Isaiah 9:10 Effect"—The attempt of a nation to defy the course of its judgment, apart from repentance, will, instead, set in motion a chain of events to bring about the very calamity it sought to avert.[1]

In the days after 9/11 Americans flocked to houses of worship to implore God's blessing on the nation. Some thought it could be the beginning of national revival, a massive return to God. But it lasted about three weeks. There was no revival. There was no repentance. And without repentance there could be no revival. In the years after 9/11 America's moral and spiritual apostasy only increased in intensity, depth, and speed.

The Seeds of Collapse

In the wake of 9/11 America attempted, as did ancient Israel, to defy the calamity, to beat back its effects, to rebuild, and to come back stronger than before. The first act of this attempt took place in the financial realm. In an effort to avoid economic catastrophe and induce recovery, the Federal Reserve began a progressive series of extreme slashings of the nation's target interest rate. This would set off a chain reaction of financial and economic repercussions that would alter the American and global economies. It would help create or spur on an explosion of credit and debt, a mortgage market boom, a housing market boom, and a stock market boom.

But the ancient principle, the Isaiah 9:10 Effect, was set in motion. The nation's attempt to defy one calamity would end up bringing about the next. It would all lead to the greatest financial collapse since the Great Depression.

When did it begin? It happened on September 17, 2001, with the first of the series of post-9/11 slashings of the nation's interest rates. *That day was Elul 29, the Day of the Shemitah.* Thus one Shemitah would set the stage for the next, and the seeds sown in one collapse would bring about the next.

Firstfruits

Since reaching bottom in the autumn of 2002, the stock market had been on a continuous and massive rise. But in 2007 a new Shemitah was nearing its start, and the ancient mystery was about to once more manifest. As its opening day drew near, there appeared more and more signs of economic danger. The rate of housing foreclosures and loan failures increased dramatically. Those institutions backing up the failed loans and mortgages found themselves in crisis. With the Shemitah's commencement just one month away, a liquidity crisis broke out in the banking industry on August 9, which some would point to as the beginning of the global crisis to come.

The first concrete sign and foreshadowing of what would soon engulf the American and global financial markets took place in Britain and yet was triggered by what was happening in America. In early September 2007 Britain's fifth-largest mortgage lender, Northern Rock, collapsed. It was the first bank run in British history in nearly one hundred fifty years. The collapse of Northern Rock has been called a "harbinger" of the global financial collapse. Indeed, many timelines of the global implosion begin with this day.

When did this first collapse take place? It happened on September 13, 2007. On the biblical calendar it was Tishri 1—the first day of the Shemitah.

What about the stock market? Was there any sign in the financial realm that the Shemitah had come? The stock market had been steadily rising for years. The Shemitah began in September 2007. On October 10 the stock market reversed its momentum and began to collapse. Not long after that, the economy fell into a recession.

The Start of the Shemitah and the Collapse of 2007

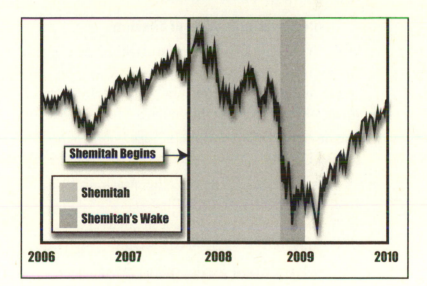

The Deepening Storm

As the Year of the Shemitah progressed, so did the stock market's collapse. In the spring of 2008 Bear Stearns, one of the most prominent global investment firms, collapsed. The signs of the Shemitah began multiplying and production decreased, as did commerce, labor, and trade. As the Shemitah progressed to its climactic end with the approach of autumn, so too the global financial crisis began rapidly escalating.

In early September the two corporations that either owned or backed half of the American mortgage market collapsed and were seized by the government in one of the most dramatic interventions since the Great Depression. With the Shemitah now two weeks away from its conclusion, the fourth-largest investment bank in America, Lehman Brothers, began to collapse. Its fall would trigger a global financial and economic implosion unseen since the days of the Great Depression.

The Seven-Year Cycle of Shakings

- The first shaking of America involved a physical destruction and collapse. The second shaking would involve destruction and collapse in the financial and economic realms.

- The mystery of the Shemitah is based on a cycle of seven years.

- The first shaking of America, the attack of 9/11, took place in the year 2001. The second shaking, the financial collapse, took place in 2008—a cycle of seven years.

- The financial collapse would happen in September 2008—a cycle of seven years to the *month* of 9/11.

- The collapse begins the second week of September—a cycle of seven years to the *week* of 9/11.

- It is as America commemorates the *seventh year* anniversary of 9/11 that the second shaking, financial implosion, is being set in motion on Wall Street.

Elul 29, 2008—
the Day of Nullification

The global financial collapse reached its peak on September 29, 2008. That morning the opening bell was struck to begin the trading day at the New York Stock Exchange—but the bell refused to ring. Observers took it as an omen. What followed the "omen" would surpass even the crash of 2001. It surpassed *every crash* in Wall Street history in magnitude. It was the greatest stock market point crash in American history. On that day the ancient mystery had again manifested.

- The greatest crash in world history took place in the Year of the Shemitah, 2008.

- It happened in September 2008, the time of the Shemitah's climactic end.

- It was connected to the biblical month of Tishri, the month of financial repercussions. The crash was sealed with the sound of ram's horns that evening as the Feast of Trumpets began.

- The crash constituted a mass nullification in the financial realm "at the end of the seventh year," the very time ordained in the Bible for the mass nullification of the financial realm.

And yet the mystery would become even more stunningly exact. When did this greatest of all stock market crashes take place? *The greatest crash in stock market history took place on Elul 29, the Day of the Shemitah—the Day of Nullification!*

The greatest financial collapse in American and world history took place on the very day given in the Bible to wipe away the financial accounts of a nation. The collapse not only fell on Elul

29, but on the one Elul 29 that comes around only once in seven years, the one twenty-four-hour period in seven years appointed for the mass nullification in a nation's financial realm.

It just happened to occur on the exact appointed day and down to the exact appointed hours in which the cancellation of financial accounts had to be accomplished. It was finished by late afternoon, before sunset, the time by which the nullification had to be completed.

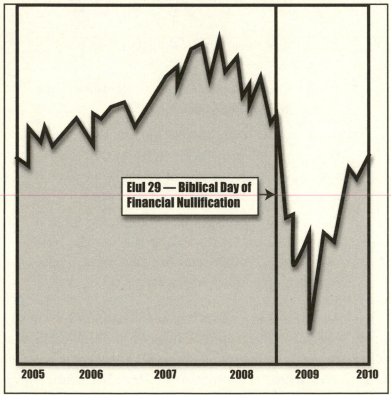

2008: Elul 29—Biblical Day of Financial Collapse

Elul 29 — Biblical Day of Financial Nullification

2005　2006　2007　2008　2009　2010

And so now again, just as it happened seven years before, the biblical Day of Nullification, on Elul 29, came the greatest nullification of financial accounts in world history.

As observant Jews around the world again nullified their financial accounts, the accounts of Wall Street were again being nullified in reality. Again the ancient mystery moved across the globe, from the New York Stock Exchange to the major stock exchanges of the world, in one vast colossal Shemitah, nullifying, canceling, wiping clean, and transforming the financial realms of the nations.

The ancient mystery had yet again manifested and could not have done so more precisely or amazingly than it did. The cycle had begun at the moment of sunset September 17, 2001, and had culminated at the moment of sunset September 29, 2008.

A Mind-Boggling Phenomenon

When one takes in the magnitude of the phenomenon, it becomes beyond stunning. It is an ancient mystery that had to have determined not only the exact timing of the two greatest stock market crashes in world history but also the timing of 9/11 itself, to name just one of the events necessary to the manifestation. All these events have impacted and altered the course of America and world history. And yet behind them lies a mystery ordained from ancient times.

On top of everything else we have seen so far, the multitude of connections and fingerprints left by the ancient mystery on the greatest financial and economic collapses of modern times is this:

- Only two stock market collapses in this millennium have borne the title of "the greatest stock market point crash in history." Both of them happened to occur on the exact same date on the biblical calendar—Elul 29.

- The day on which they each took place just happens to have been ordained in the writings of Scripture from ancient times.

- They each took place on a day that comes up only once in several years.

- This once-in-several-years occurrence happens to be the same day that is specifically ordained from ancient times in Scripture as the day of a mass nullification in the financial realm—the very thing that took place on Wall Street on that exact day.

- The ancient mystery determines that this mass nullification of financial accounts take place exactly seven biblical years apart. The two greatest crashes not only took place on Elul 29, but on Elul 29 exactly seven biblical years apart, down to the day.

2000–2001 & 2007–2008

The Two Shemitahs and the Two Global Collapses

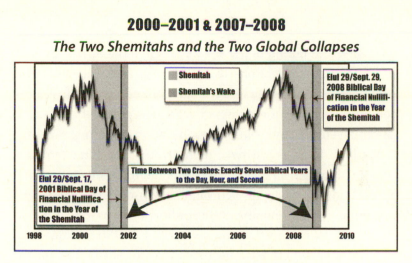

The Phenomenon of 2,569 Days

If we let the phenomenon speak for itself, it reveals a clear message. The crash that had been triggered by the events of 9/11 assumed the title of the greatest stock market point collapse in history on September 17, 2001. It happened on the day appointed in the Bible for the mass nullification of financial accounts. The ancient mystery ordained that seven years after the first event will come a recurrence of that event, another mass nullification of financial accounts. These are seven biblical, lunar-solar, Hebrew years.

According to the ancient mystery, the time period ordained for the second event to take place is 2,569 days. The collapse of 2008 took place exactly 2,569 days after the first, as ordained from ancient times. The first crash would carry the title of the greatest stock market collapse in history for exactly 2,569 days, the exact number ordained in the ancient mystery. It would then be transcended by the second collapse, which took place on the exact same Hebrew day appointed from ancient times.

An Unseen Hand

The rising and falling of the stock market is the result of countless financial transactions in markets throughout the world, countless developments in the financial and economic realms colliding with countless human reactions, interactions, calculations, feelings, and whims—each action affecting the next. No human hand could have orchestrated anything remotely approaching such a phenomenon. It could have only transpired by the moving of an unseen hand. Its complexity combined with its precision remains nothing short of mind-boggling.

It is worth noting that the mystery of the Shemitah, in its last two manifestations, appears to have intensified in magnitude and precision, an intensification that parallels an intensification and acceleration in the spiritual and moral descent of America and much of the modern world.

The phenomenon is overwhelming. The mystery of the Shemitah has affected the course of the stock market and the economy, America and the nations, and the lives of everyone reading these words.

And even this is not the end. We are going to find that the ancient mystery operates in ways one would never expect and in realms one would never have imagined. And, of course, it will speak of things yet to come.

————————————

Before entering into another realm of the mystery, we will unlock one last revelation concerning the realm of crashes— a revelation involving one of the most mysterious, if not mystical, chain of events.

Chapter 15

The MYSTERY of SEVENS

The Number of the Shemitah

WOVEN INTO THE mystery of the Shemitah is the number seven. The Shemitah is the seventh year and the conclusion of a seven-year cycle.

Seven is also the number of the remission brought about by the Shemitah. When, on Elul 29, the financial realm is wiped clean, the debts and credits that are nullified are those of the past seven years. So the effect of the Shemitah extends seven years into the past, the entire seven-year cycle. The Shemitah is the Sabbath of years. And just as seven is the number of the Sabbath, seven is also the number of the Shemitah.

Is it possible that the greatest stock market point crash in history, having taken place on the Day of the Shemitah, would bear the marks of the Sabbath year—in the form of the number seven?

The following is not central nor essential to the phenomenon or mystery of the Shemitah—but it is a fascinating phenomenon in its own right.

The Mark of Seven

- **The Seven-Year Mark:** The greatest point crash in stock market history happened on Elul 29—the end of the *seventh year* and the completion of the *seven-year cycle.*

- **The Seventh Month:** On the evening of the greatest crash began the month of Tishri. Tishri is the seventh month of the sacred calendar. Thus the crash took place on the day that ushers in the most sacred of times in the biblical calendar, *the seventh month.*

- **Seven Hundred Billion:** The crash was triggered by the failure of Congress to pass the Emergency Economic Stabilization Act. The bill was a response to the economic implosion of September 2008, an attempt to save the US financial system. The amount chosen for the bailout was *seven hundred billion* dollars.

- **Seven Percent—2008:** What percentage of Wall Street was wiped out on the last day of the seventh year? *Seven percent.*

- **Seven Percent—2001:** How much of Wall Street was wiped out seven years earlier on the last day of the preceding Shemitah in 2001? *Seven percent.*

- **Seven-Seven-Seven:** How many actual points were wiped out on the last day of the seventh year? *Seven hundred seventy-seven (777).*

The Timekeeper

When the kingdom of Judah was destroyed in 586 BC, few of the survivors could have fathomed what lay ahead. The land was depopulated in a mass deportation of Judeans to an exile in Babylon. The most likely scenario was that there would never again be a Jewish nation in the land of Israel. But what the future actually held was dramatically different.

The secret of what would take place and of exactly when it would take place was already there, contained in the mystery of the Shemitah. The Babylonian exile would last for seventy years based on the timing determined by the seventy Shemitah years the nation had broken. Once those years were completed, the exiles would return.

The Shemitah held the secret to the timing of the nation's judgment.

The Shemitah had always been linked to timing. And its timing was always linked to the number seven. In 586 BC when the Shemitah moved into the realm of prophetic signs and national judgment, its manifestation followed the number seven—seventy years of desolation, years representing seven-year cycles, the period in which the Shemitahs were broken—a chain of sevens through time.

A Journey of Sevens

What would happen if we now embarked on a journey beginning from the Shemitah's climactic end and following a mystery of sevens backward through time? Specifically, what if we began this journey in the last hours of the last day of the last Shemitah—at the end of the greatest stock market point crash, just as it hits the number 777? It is September 29, 2008. The time is 4:00 p.m. The closing bell rings. The crash is finished. We now follow a chain of sevens back in time.

First Sequence: The Chain of Years

From the closing bell of the crash we go back in time seven years—seven exact biblical years, down to the hour. Where does it bring us?

It brings us to Monday, September 17, 2001, the day of the other greatest point crash in American history. More precisely, it brings us to 4:00 p.m., to the closing bell, to the very last moment of the other collapse. Seven Hebrew years have taken us from the closing bell and final minute of the one crash to the closing bell and final minute of the other.

Second Sequence: The Chain of Days

Now from that seven-year mark, and the closing bell of the crash of 2001, we follow the chain of sevens back in time once more—seven days—to the seventh day. From 4:00 p.m. Monday to 4:00 p.m. Sunday we have the first twenty-four-hour period, the first day. The chain then proceeds according to this sequence:

- From 4:00 p.m. Sunday to 4:00 p.m. Saturday—the second day

- From 4:00 p.m. Saturday to 4:00 p.m. Friday—the third day

- From 4:00 p.m. Friday to 4:00 p.m. Thursday—the fourth day

- From 4:00 p.m. Thursday to 4:00 p.m. Wednesday—the fifth day

- From 4:00 p.m. Wednesday to 4:00 p.m. Tuesday—the sixth day

The seventh day, going back in time, begins at four o'clock Tuesday afternoon. Is this significant? It could not be more so. *The seventh day is September 11, 2001.*

So the seventh day in its entirety, proceeding backward in time, would begin at 4:00 p.m. Tuesday (September 11). The time period would include Tuesday afternoon, Tuesday morning, Monday evening (September 10), and late afternoon. It is in the midst of these hours that the attack of 9/11 will take place. The mystery of sevens has brought us back not only to the minute of the stock market crash of 2001, but also to the day of the attack, 9/11.

Third Sequence: The Chain of Hours

Now what happens if we follow the chain of sevens once more—seven hours? Starting at 4:00 p.m. Tuesday afternoon, September 11, and going back in time seven hours:

- From 4:00 p.m. to 3:00 p.m.—the first hour

- From 3:00 p.m. to 2:00 p.m.—the second hour

- From 2:00 p.m. to 1:00 p.m.—the third hour

- From 1:00 p.m. to 12:00 p.m.—the fourth hour
- From 12:00 p.m. to 11:00 a.m.—the fifth hour
- From 11:00 a.m. to 10:00 a.m.—the sixth hour

The seventh hour falls on Tuesday morning, between 9:00 and 10:00 a.m. Is this significant? Yes. This is the key time period of 9/11. As the hour approaches, the first tower is hit. At the beginning of the hour, the second tower is hit. And just before the hour is over, the first of the two towers will have collapsed. The mystery of sevens has brought us back to the very morning and hour of 9/11.

The two strikes happen within a space of seventeen minutes. The end of the seven hours brings us to 9:00 a.m., and 9:00 a.m. falls within the seventeen minutes between the strikes.

Fourth Sequence: The Chain of Minutes

What happens if we follow the mystery of sevens into the realm of minutes? The mystery has already led us to 9:00 a.m. The crash of the second plane into the South Tower happens at 9:03 a.m. So the chain of sevens has taken us from the crash of Wall Street in 2008 to a point in time less than five minutes from the attack.

If we now go back two more cycles of seven, cycles of seven minutes, we end up at 8:46 a.m., the minute in which the first strike takes place—the exact moment 9/11 began.

From the Closing Bell to the Time of the Strike

Starting from the biblical "end of the seventh year," the Shemitah's climax, the mystery has taken us from the number 777 and the closing bell of one stock market collapse to the closing bell of the other. From there it has brought us to the

day of September 11, 2001—and then to the hour of the attack—
and then to the period of minutes in between the two attacks.

The Mystery of Sevens

The mystery of the Shemitah involves the striking of a nation's
financial and economic realms. And yet, as we have seen, it
can extend beyond these realms to involve national calamities,
even attacks on cities and nations, as it did in 586 BC and as it
did on September 11, 2001. And the timing of these calamities
is contained within the Shemitah's mystery of sevens—in both
586 BC and AD 2001.

Between the crash of 2008 and the attack of 9/11 are 2,575
days. Within those days are 3,708,000 minutes. And yet the
mystery pinpoints America's greatest crashes and the attack of
9/11 down to the minutes—if not to the very minute.

And even without the mystery of sevens we have three of the
most dramatic shakings in recent history, 9/11 and the collapse
of Wall Street in 2001 and 2008, all connected to the mystery of
the Shemitah—not only in their timing but in their origins. The
crash at the end of the Shemitah of 2008 was linked to the crash
at the end of the Shemitah in 2001. That crash, in turn, was linked
to what happened on 9/11. In view of all this, we must once again
take note of the Shemitah's specific prophetic meaning—as the
sign of judgment to a nation that has driven God out of its life
and brought in idols and gods of increase in His place. In such a
scenario the sign appears as warning of things to come.

We are now about to enter a new realm within the mystery of
the Shemitah—a realm so different that one might wonder how
it could be connected at all. And yet, as we will see, it is strangely
connected and concerns the rise and fall of nations up to our day.

PART V

THE SHEMITAH
AND
THE MYSTERY
OF THE
TOWERS

Chapter 16

The FIRST TOWER

Towers

Towers have risen from the center points of civilization from the days of Egypt and Mesopotamia onward. From the beginning of recorded history they have stood as symbols of kingdoms, empires, cities, and cultures—embodiments of man's aspirations, monuments to the greatness and glory of the powers that produced them.

The Migdalim

Though, in Scripture, towers can stand as symbols of strength and glory, they often stand as symbols of pride. The very first tower mentioned in the Bible is the most famous of all towers and their archetype—the Tower of Babel:

> And they said, "Come, let us build ourselves a city, and a tower whose top is in the heavens; let us make a name for ourselves…"
>
> —GENESIS 11:4

The account is filled with far-reaching themes and ramifications.

- The first is the theme of civilization. The tower isn't built in a desert but appears within a specific context. First comes the city and then the tower. Towers are linked to civilization. They stand as symbols of the civilizations out of which they arise.

- The second is the theme of greatness. By building the tower, the people intend to make a name for themselves. The tower is the embodiment of man's aspiration for greatness.

- The third theme will come into play further on.

The word for towers in Hebrew is *migdalim*, the plural of *migdal*. The word *migdal* comes from the Hebrew root word *gadal*, which can be translated as:

- "To increase"
- "To be lifted up"

- "To be promoted"
- "To wax great"
- "To be magnified"
- "To be enlarged"
- "To become great"

In Hebrew, even the word for towers is linked to greatness. This parallels the age-old function of towers as monuments and testaments of greatness. Even in our day the greatest of towers invariably function in some way as symbols of greatness.

In the past thousand years of history cathedrals constituted the tallest man-made structures on the earth. Accordingly, for most of this period, the institutionalized church of Europe constituted one of the greatest centers of power on the earth. But in the latter part of the past thousand years cathedrals have been replaced by secular buildings as the tallest man-made structures or buildings on the earth. The towers reveal a massive shift from ecclesiastical power to secular power.

Considering the connection of towers to greatness, and the connection in biblical Hebrew, could the rising of towers reflect the "lifting up," the "waxing great," or the rise to greatness of nations?

The World's First Skyscraper

In the nineteenth century a new way of building was developed. Instead of using walls to bear the building's weight, the building would be supported by an internal skeletal structure of iron or steel. This was not only more practical, but it also allowed for buildings to rise higher than ever before, paving the way for the creation of the skyscraper.

In the late 1860s construction began on what is considered by many to be the world's first skyscraper. It would be built on American soil. It was called the Equitable Life Assurance Building. It is considered the first building in the world to combine great heights, usable stories, a lightweight fireproof construction, and an interior skeletal metal frame. It was also the first office building in the world to have passenger elevators. It was built in New York City at 120 Broadway. It was also the tallest non-cathedral building on the earth. And its rising would not be an isolated phenomenon—but the beginning of many such tall buildings.

The Rising Tower and the Changing of World Power

In view of the biblical connection of towers to increase, greatness, and rising, is it possible that the rising of this unprecedented tower in New York City is connected to a parallel changing and transference of world power?

The rise of what some consider the world's first skyscraper in New York City signaled the end of Europe's reign as the land of the tallest buildings on earth. The tower, which stood at 120 Broadway, heralded the age when American towers would reign supreme over every building on the earth, no matter what type or kind.

Did this change in the world's towers reflect a shifting in world power as well? If so, the change would reflect a shift from the old world to the new. Did any such change take place?

In the last decades of the nineteenth century a dramatic transformation took place in the world. The period saw the rise of America's industrial economy, large-scale agriculture, big business, and the largest economic expansion in American history. When did it begin?

The year recognized as its starting point is 1870—the same year that the American tower was completed. The tower marked the beginning of the "Gilded Age," the nation's massive transformation into an industrial power. The rise of the tower coincided with the rise of American world power.

Even more specifically, the tower was completed in the middle of 1870, on May 1. Behind the scenes a change was taking place. The change would profoundly alter the course of world history for the next century and beyond. The year that marked this colossal change began seven months after the tower was finished.

In 1871 America overtook the British Empire to become the nation with the largest economy on the earth. One of the meanings of *gadal*, from which the Hebrew word for tower comes, is "to be made large." And that is exactly what happened. In 1870 the tower was finished. By 1871 America had become the greatest economic power on earth. It had been enlarged, lifted up, and made great.

This changing of world power in 1870–1871 would produce far-reaching repercussions in world history. It would determine the course of the First World War, the Great Depression, the Second World War, the Cold War, and the modern age as we know it.

The Rise of the Towers

The tower of 1870 marked the beginning of a new era. It marked not only America's emergence as the strongest economic power on the earth but also America's preeminence with regard to towers. From the moment of its completion onward, America would be the land of the tallest buildings on the earth. It would hold this distinction for over a century, continuously and with no serious challengers. As the tallest towers on the earth continued to rise on American soil, so too America itself would continue to rise in power and preeminence on the world stage.

As the twentieth century progressed, the ancient mystery linking *migdal*, the tower, to *gadal*, greatness, would continue to manifest. The rising of the towers would parallel the rising of American world power. And just as the American towers were reaching heights never before attained in human history, so too America itself was reaching heights of power no nation or empire in world history had ever attained.

The mystery of the towers, which began in the ancient Middle East, was now manifesting in the modern world and on American soil. The mystery stood at the center of the most massive shifting of world power in modern history. It stood behind the emergence of what would be known as "the American century." And its repercussions would touch every part of the globe.

But as the twentieth century approached its end, there would be a new development in the mystery. And that change would have profound ramifications concerning our day and the future of America and the world.

As we move toward these ramifications and what they reveal concerning the future, we must first answer a question: What does the mystery of the towers have to do with the Shemitah?

Chapter 17

The FOUR TOWERS

The Days of the High Towers

B EGINNING WITH ITS rise to economic superpower and throughout the twentieth century, America erected the tallest towers on the earth, ever higher and higher. At the dawn of the twentieth century it would build the tallest building of any kind, surpassing the Ulm Cathedral in Germany. And then, at the beginning of the 1930s, it would erect the largest man-made structure, skyscraper or otherwise, on the planet.

Paralleling America's rise to world power was the rise of New York City. As America became the greatest power on earth, New York City would become the chief of cities. In the twentieth century the city would become the world's financial center, the world's cultural center, and, in the eyes of many, the world's capital—the center point of world power.

According to the mystery, it should not surprise us that in this same period it should also become the city with the highest towers on the earth. A disproportionate amount of the world's highest buildings would now rise up from its pavement. Through much of the twentieth century it could boast of having eleven of the world's tallest buildings.

As America's towers attained greater and greater heights, so did the nation's powers. America's rise on the world stage would be dramatically propelled and accelerated by two world wars. Between the wars, in the center of the period, there would be an unprecedented explosion of activity in the construction of the world's tallest towers. It would take place in the years 1930 and 1931. In that short space of time no less than four different structures held the mantle of the world's tallest building—all of them in America, all in New York City.

The period of 1930–1931 bore another distinction. It was the time of the Shemitah.

The First Three Towers

The first of the four towers was the Woolworth Building—completed in 1913, just before the start of the First World War, it stood at 791 feet.

In the spring of 1930 it was surpassed by the second tower, the Bank of Manhattan Trust Building, which attained a height of 928 feet. Its reign would be short-lived. Less than thirty days after its completion it was surpassed by the third tower.

Upon its completion in May of 1930, the Chrysler Building became not only the world's tallest building but also, in surpassing the Eiffel Tower in France, the tallest man-made structure on the planet. It was also the first man-made structure on the earth to exceed a height of 1,000 feet.

In the year 1930, in the timing of the Shemitah's approach, three different towers bore the crown of the world's tallest building. But when the Shemitah commenced, it would herald the greatest of the four towers and that which would become one of the most famous buildings ever erected by human hands.

The Fourth Tower

The Empire State Building was begun in January of 1930 and completed in the spring of 1931, in the midst of the Shemitah of 1930–1931. It would rise to a height of 1,250 feet at its top floor and 1,454 feet at the top of its spire. The completion of the Empire State Building would mark the end of the most intense period of rising towers in human history. No other building would rival its height for years to come. It would reign as the world's tallest building for four decades, longer than any other building in the twentieth century.

The Empire State Building would become an American and global icon. It would be called "the eighth wonder of the world." It would stand as a symbol not only of human achievement, but, specifically, of American achievement. It would embody the soaring heights, the unprecedented power, and the unparalleled magnitude that American civilization had now attained.

It was a fitting symbol for what was about to take place. With the advent of the Second World War America would be lifted up to heights of power no nation had ever known. And the tower that stood in the midst of its greatest city would become the most visible and potent symbol of that rising and of those heights.

With the end of the Second World War, New York City was exploding with celebrations of victory. It was a new era in which America would be the head of nations. In the midst of the celebrations stood the nation's soaring tower, dominating the city's skyline and bearing witness of the ancient connect linking a civilization's tower to its greatness.

The Tower and the Shemitah

The connection of the Empire State Building to the biblical Shemitah was not just one of timing but of circumstance. At the time of its rising, America was in a state of financial and economic collapse. The tower was built in the depths of the Great Depression.

The contrast could not have been more jarring—a nation sinking into the abyss of economic collapse and a colossal tower rising from its midst. It was because of the Great Depression that, a year after its completion, the Empire State Building remained overwhelmingly empty. The tower boasted of America's glory, the greatness of its powers, the vastness of its resources, and the heights of its rising. The Depression, on the other hand, spoke a different message. It testified of a nation's weakness, its poverty, its inabilities, and the collapse of its prosperity. America would ultimately recover from the Depression and continue its long rise to the heights of world power. But the connection binding together the rising of the nation's towers and the Shemitah would continue.

There would, in future days, arise another building that would, likewise, boast of the nation's greatness. But, as we will see, the mystery of the Shemitah would frame its rising. While towers, by nature, speak of power and glory, the Shemitah speaks of something very different. It reminds a nation that its blessings and powers come only from God. And, without God, they must fall.

The Towers and the Day of Warning

The Harbinger reveals a prophetic warning given to America at its first full day as a fully formed nation. The warning parallels the message of the Shemitah. It was, in effect, this: America's blessings come from God. If the nation should ever turn away from God and reject His ways, then the blessings of God would be removed from the land.

The Harbinger reveals the date on which the warning was given, April 30, 1789.[1] The date will reappear in the mystery of the towers, particularly in the key years of 1930 and 1931. The reign of the first of the four towers came to its end on April 30, 1931, the anniversary of the prophetic warning. The second tower was not only completed on the anniversary of the warning but was also erected on the same ground on which that warning was given. The reign of the second tower ended soon after with the completion of the third tower that same spring. The third tower would stand as the tallest building on the earth for one year. Its reign would, in turn, come to an end on the same date, April 30, the date of the prophetic warning. For it was on April 30 that the Empire State Building became the tallest building on earth.

The Last Tower

Years later, after the World Trade Center was destroyed on 9/11, the Empire State Building would again stand preeminent as the tallest building in the New York skyline. In 2012 the rising tower of Ground Zero finally surpassed the Empire State Building to become the tallest building on the New York skyline. On what day did that happen? It took place on the date given in *The Harbinger*, April 30, which had been released four months earlier. The Empire State Building was surpassed on the exact same date on which it had surpassed the Chrysler Building as the tallest building on the earth. The Chrysler Building had, in turn, become the world's tallest building after surpassing the previous title holder, which had been completed as well on that same date—the date on which the prophetic warning had been given to America.

So each of the four towers had either begun its reign or ended its reign on the date of the prophetic message, when America was warned against turning away from God. Now the fifth tower had ascended past the Empire State Building on the same date as well.

The mystery of the towers is linked to a national warning—and to the Shemitah. The towers boasted of the soaring heights to which American civilization had risen. But the Shemitah reminds a nation that all of its blessings come from God, and without Him they cannot remain. The prophetic message warned similarly that if America ever turned away from God, those blessings would come to an end.

With the completion of the Empire State Building in 1931, the days of the high towers would come to a close—until the rise of the World Trade Center. So too the Shemitah, in which the final and tallest of America's high towers rose, would also come to an end. Its end came, of course, on Elul 29. But on the

Western calendar—the Shemitah that ended the time of the high towers was September 11.

———————

As America assumed the mantle of "head of nations," the mystery of the towers would carry even more critical and prophetic consequence. There would arise another building, made up of two towers. It would take the crown away from the Empire State Building. In its rising, the mystery of the Shemitah and the mystery of the towers would converge. And its fall would signal the beginning of the harbingers and the warning days of national judgment.

Chapter 18

The TOWERS of HEGEMON

The American Apogee

THE YEAR WAS 1945. America had emerged from the Second World War having attained a unique position described in the Scriptures over three thousand years earlier as "the head of nations." Its navies patrolled the world's waters, its currency undergirded the world's financial system, the fruit of its commerce and culture saturated the earth, and its military carried out America's assumed role as the "world's policeman." It had achieved a level of relative power and global hegemony unprecedented in world history.

The ancient connection between a nation's greatness and the building of towers would now argue for the erection of a new edifice that would embody America's role as the head of nations and the central pillar of the new global order. Could there now arise a tower or towers linked to America's new apogee of world power?

The Conception

In July 1944, anticipating the end of the Second World War, representatives of forty-four nations gathered in Bretton Woods, New Hampshire, to lay the foundation for a new global economic order based on the American dollar and for the reconstruction of national economies devastated by the war. The answer, they believed, was to expand international trade. And America would be the world trade center of the new era.

In 1945, the year of the war's end and America's rise to superpower, David Scholz, former governor of Florida and real estate developer, first proposed the concept of "a world trade center" in Lower Manhattan near Wall Street to encourage trade and port activity in the city. The plan was part of a series of projects aimed at encouraging world trade and solidifying America's role in the new world order.

In 1946 the New York State legislature authorized the creation of the World Trade Corporation to develop the World Trade Center. That same year funds were given to purchase land along the East River on which to build the United Nations Headquarters, also in New York City. Both projects would affirm America's new position as world center.

The World Trade Center was conceived in 1945 at America's apogee of power—1945 was also the Year of the Shemitah.

The Construction

In 1958 David Rockefeller produced a master plan for the transformation of Lower Manhattan. The plan included an office complex dedicated to world trade. In November of that same year Nelson Rockefeller was elected governor of New York. In 1961 the World Trade Center bill was signed by Governor Rockefeller and New Jersey governor Richard Hughes. A new site was proposed for the trade center, a sixteen-acre lot of land along the Hudson River.

In March 1966 the New York State Court of Appeals dismissed the last legal challenge to the World Trade Center. This cleared the way for the construction to start. According to the plans, the World Trade Center would consist of two central towers. On March 21, 1966, demolition began to clear the thirteen square blocks of low-rise buildings in Radio Row. On August 5, 1966, a giant concrete wall was sunk into the ground as part of the groundbreaking—1966 was also the Year of the Shemitah.

The Shemitah began on September 27, 1965, and reached its conclusion on September 14, 1966. In the middle of the Shemitah the work commences on what will be the ground of construction. And before the Shemitah draws to its end, the building begins.

Thus the construction of the World Trade Center is begun in the Year of the Shemitah.

The Completion

Steel work began on the center's North Tower in August 1968 and on the South Tower in January 1969. On December 23, 1970, the final columns of the North Tower were set into place on the 110th floor. In July 1971 a topping-off ceremony was held on the South Tower.

In 1972, with the upper stories of the North Tower now completed, the Empire State Building's forty-year reign came to an end. The World Trade Center became the tallest building on the earth.

The World Trade Center and its twin towers were officially finished and inaugurated in a dedication and ribbon-cutting ceremony held by the Port Authority on April 4, 1973—1973 was also the Year of the Shemitah.

The Shemitah had commenced on September 9, 1972. It would conclude on September 26, 1973. That same year the World Trade Center surpassed the Empire State Building to become the tallest building on the earth. As for 1973, it was the year the twin towers were officially completed and dedicated, in April, in the center of the Shemitah.

Thus the World Trade Center was finished and dedicated in the Year of the Shemitah.

The Destruction

On a warm and nearly cloudless day in September 2001 at 8:46 in the morning, American Airlines Flight 11, a Boeing 767, struck the North Tower of the World Trade Center. Nearly seventeen minutes later, at 9:03 a.m., United Airlines Flight 175, another Boeing 767, struck the South Tower. At 9:59 a.m. the South Tower collapsed into a vast rolling cloud of dust, and at 10:28 a.m. the North Tower collapsed.

That which had once stood as the tallest building on earth was no more. That which had been conceived at the same moment in history in which America assumed its mantle of world superpower now had vanished in a cloud of white dust. And that which had stood as a monument to America's global preeminence and to the American-led world order now lay in ruins. The year 2001 marked the fall of the World Trade Center—2001 was also the Year of the Shemitah.

The Shemitah had begun on September 30, 2000. It would conclude on September 17, 2001. September 11 took place on Elul 23 on the ancient calendar, in the last climactic week of the Shemitah. Thus the World Trade Center was destroyed in the Year of the Shemitah.

The Two Mysteries

We have the mystery of the Shemitah and the mystery of the towers converging in the World Trade Center and leading up to the day on which the towers fell in September 2001. The connections linking the World Trade Center to the ancient mystery are remarkable in their consistency. The World Trade Center was:

- Conceived in the Shemitah of 1945

- Begun in the Shemitah of 1966

- Built in a seven-year period beginning and ending in the Year of the Shemitah

- Finished and dedicated in the Shemitah of 1973

- Destroyed in the Shemitah of 2001

But what is behind this phenomenon? And what is its meaning and its message—or its warning—to America and the world?

Chapter 19

The MYSTERY of the TOWERS

The Vow

WHAT IS THE connection between the mystery of the Shemitah and that of the towers—and what is its meaning?

For the answer we must return to the ancient vow spoken after the attack on the land, Israel's first massive warning of coming judgment. Here now is the context of that vow:

> The LORD sent a word against Jacob, and it has fallen on
> Israel. All the people will know—Ephraim and the inhab-
> itant of Samaria—who say in pride and arrogance of
> heart: "The bricks have fallen down, but we will rebuild
> with hewn stones…"
>
> —ISAIAH 9:8–10

The vow is introduced with the words: *"Who say in pride
and arrogance of heart…"* What does this have to do with the
mystery of the towers? The connection isn't visible in English.
But it appears in the original Hebrew.

The Godel Connection

In the original language the word translated as "arrogance" is
the Hebrew *godel*. *Godel* can be translated either as "greatness"
or "arrogance." It comes from the root word *gadal*. We have
seen this word before. *Gadal* is the same word from which
we get *migdal*, the Hebrew word for tower. Likewise, the word
gadal not only speaks of magnitude, enlargement, and greatness, but also of arrogance, boasting, and pride. So a tower
can symbolize a civilization's magnitude, enlargement, and
greatness—but it can also symbolize its arrogance, its boasting,
and its pride.

This is doubly striking since the mystery of *The Harbinger*
connects the ancient vow of Isaiah 9:10, spoken in the wake of
the ancient attack, with the destruction of the towers in the
attack on 9/11. And in the original Hebrew the word describing
the arrogance in which this vow is spoken is linked to the
Hebrew word for tower—the very object destroyed on 9/11.

The Spirit of Babel

The connection between towers and pride was there in the very first tower recorded in Scripture and in the words by which its rising began:

> Come, let us build ourselves a city, and a tower whose top is in the heavens; let us make a name for ourselves...
> —GENESIS 11:4

This is the third theme embodied by towers—the theme of pride. The Tower of Babel's purpose was to enable its builders to "make a name" for themselves. How? By erecting "a tower whose top is in the heavens." The Tower of Babel was man's endeavor to ascend to heaven by his own will and powers, his striving to equal God. Babel was man's attempt at godhood. It was built in the same spirit of defiance as that which infused the rebuilding in Isaiah 9:10.

But this brings up another theme. The building of the Tower of Babel brings judgment. The rebuilding of Isaiah 9:10 will also bring judgment. A tower may become the embodiment of pride and arrogance. And in such a case a tower may become the focal point of judgment.

The Tower and the Shemitah:
The Meaning of the Mysteries

What is the connection between the mystery of the Shemitah and that of the towers?

Towers are symbols of greatness and often of pride.
The Shemitah acts to break man's pride, humble a nation, and bring humility.

Towers stand as monuments to the power and glory of man or of a civilization.

The Shemitah reminds man of his weakness or a nation of its total dependence on God.

Towers stand as testaments of a nation's prosperity and wealth.

The Shemitah reminds that nation that the source of its blessings come from God, and without Him those blessings cannot remain.

Towers boast of man's claims of dominion and sovereignty.

The Shemitah calls man to relinquish his claims of dominion and sovereignty before the sovereignty and dominion of God.

A tower rises.

The Shemitah is about letting…fall.

A tower may embody a nation's rise to power.

The Shemitah in the form of judgment is linked to the fall of such a nation.

A tower represents a building up.

The Shemitah brings about the wiping away of what has been built up.

A tower manifests the pursuit of height, the goal of rising higher and higher away from the foundation.

The Shemitah manifests a return to the foundation.

When the judgment of God fell on the land of Israel, that which the nation built up was wiped away, and its buildings were leveled.

When the Shemitah comes, that which the nation has built up in its financial and economic realms is wiped away. It levels accounts and brings back to ground level all that has been built up in the years before its coming.

A fall of a tower may come in the form of a crash or collapse.

The impact of the Shemitah on the financial realm brings about that which, in effect, constitutes a fall, a collapse, and a crash.

The Shamat

The word *shemitah* comes from the Hebrew root word *shamat. Shamat* can be translated as "to release" and "to remit," as in the release or remission of debts in the Year of the Shemitah. It can also mean "to let alone," as in no longer watching over or maintaining that which had been watched over and maintained. It can signify the releasing of one's grip to allow the natural course of things to progress and the natural consequences to fall. It can also mean "to detach" and "to pull away." It can also mean "to loosen." And it can mean "to shake," "to overthrow," "to cast down," "to discontinue," "to let fall," or "collapse."

All these things can be applied to the ordinance of the Shemitah. The people were to release and let go of their claims of ownership, to let fall their accounts of credit and debts, and to detach from their land and leave it to its natural course.

But when the Shemitah manifests in the form of judgment, all these things take on new meaning and new manifestations. In 586 BC the Shemitah manifested in the form of judgment. God "released His grip" on the nation; He "pulled away" and withdrew His protection. The armies of Babylon then overran its borders. The nation was shaken to its foundation. It was allowed to fall. It was overthrown, cast down. The kingdom collapsed. It was discontinued. This was the Shemitah, or the *shamat*, in the form of judgment.

"Upon Every High Tower"

It is striking that one of the biblical signs of judgment is the striking down of that which is lifted up and the casting down of that which is high and lofty:

> For the day of the LORD of hosts shall come upon every-thing proud and lofty, upon everything lifted up—and it shall be brought low...*upon every high tower*...
> —ISAIAH 2:12–15,
> *EMPHASIS ADDED*

From ancient times to the modern world, that which is most "lifted up" and that which is most "proud and lofty" is the tower. Therefore one of the clearest biblical signs of a nation under judgment is the casting down of its "high towers."

The Days of Glory's End

We have seen the ancient connection between towers and greatness, and between the first high tower of the modern age and the rising of America as a world power. The year in which the two converged, 1870, was the beginning of a new era. The highest towers on the earth continued to rise on American soil just as America itself continued to rise on the world stage. From 1870 and through most of the twentieth century, every building holding the title of being the tallest in the world had been erected on American soil. The majority of these had risen in the nation's Empire City: New York.

But as the twentieth century drew to its close, a change took place; the age of America as the land of the highest towers on the earth came to an end. The world's tallest buildings were now being built on other lands. In 1998 the Petronas Towers in Malaysia surpassed the height of the highest American tower to become the tallest building on earth. In 2003 the Taipei World Financial Center in China surpassed the Petronas Towers to become the world's highest tower. And in 2010 the Burj Khalifa in the United Arab Emirates surpassed the Taipei World Financial Center to become the tallest building on earth. The age when America's towers soared above every other was over. What had begun in the nineteenth century was now over. The tallest buildings of the new millennium were now ascending on Asian soil.

What about the ancient link of towers and greatness? If the rise of the world's first skyscraper marked America's rise, if the continuous ascent of the world's tallest buildings on American land marked America's continuous rise to unprecedented heights of world power—then what did it now mean that America's highest towers were now being eclipsed by those of other lands and nations? What did it portend?

The above citing of the world's tallest buildings is based on the height of the highest architectural element in each building. If one uses a different criterion, that of the height of the building's tip, including its antenna, then the World Trade Center remained the tallest building in America to the end of the century. In fact, it remained the tallest building in the world. Its reign then only ended in the year 2000. It was a significant year in which to end. For 2000 was the year in which began the Shemitah.

The Mystery of the Shemitah
and the Fall of the Towers

To the nation that has driven the God it had once known out of its life, rejected His ways, defied His will, and hardened itself to His calling, the Shemitah manifests in the form of judgment. As it entered the third millennium, America was such a nation. The Shemitah began in September 2000 and reached its climactic conclusion in September of 2001. If the Shemitah were to manifest in America as a sign of judgment, how would that sign of judgment manifest in September of 2001?

In view of what Shemitah can mean, what if, in the Year of the Shemitah 2001, God "let alone" the nation that had so driven Him out of its life, out of its culture, and out of its public squares? What if God "released His grip" on the United States, if He "pulled away" His protection from that nation, even for a moment? What if He allowed a nation, which had so hardened and deafened itself to the calling of His voice, to now be "shaken"?

The September Mysteries

The events of September 11, 2001, took place in the last climactic week of the Shemitah. In that week it all came together, the mystery of the towers and the mystery of the Shemitah. The twin towers would collapse as the Shemitah moved to its climactic end. What happens when the two mysteries converge? We have the tower, that which stands as a symbol of a nation's greatness and the embodiment of its pride. And we have the Shemitah, that which humbles the pride of a nation and that which reminds a nation that without God, all its blessings and powers must fail. The tower speaks of rising. The Shemitah speaks of falling and wiping away that which has been built up.

The tower rises far from its foundation. The Shemitah brings all things back to the foundation. According to the ancient mystery and the words of the prophets, on the Day of Judgment, that which is "proud and lofty" is humbled, that which is "lifted up" is brought low, and that which is "exalted" is cast down. The day of calamity specifically comes against "the high towers" of the land. On that day of a nation's judgment its high towers fall. On September 11, 2001, in the days of the Shemitah's climax, America's high towers were cast down.

In September of 2001 the effect of the Shemitah, as revealed in its root word, *shamat*, was manifested. It was America's day of shaking. It was the day when that which had been built up was wiped away. On September 11, 2001, America's high towers were "allowed to fall." The World Trade Center was "cast down." Its soaring twin towers "collapsed" into dust.

It all took place within days of the seventh year's end when the Shemitah's impact strikes the financial realm—the Day of Remission, when financial accounts are wiped clean. That would come the following Monday with the greatest stock market point collapse in Wall Street history.

The Shemitah's Two Collapses

When the Bible speaks of Elul 29, the Day of Remission, the word used is *shamat*. That word also describes what happened to the financial realm on Elul 29, 2001. A great "pulling away" took place on Wall Street. The world's financial markets were shaken. Fortunes were "cast down." Wall Street was "allowed to fall." And the world's financial realm "collapsed."

The Two Crashes

If one looks at a graph of the New York Stock Exchange in the years of the last two Shemitahs, one will find two great peaks.

The picture resembles mountaintops or something of a skyline of pointed skyscrapers.

The Wiping Away of Heights

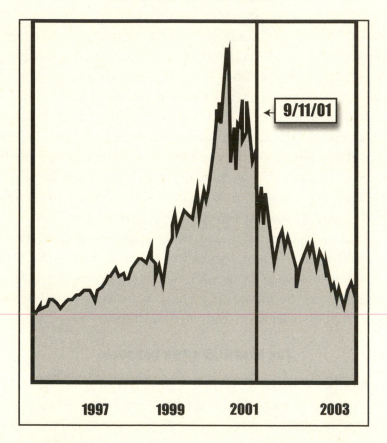

Judgment involves the casting down of that which has been lifted. The Shemitah involves the wiping away of that which has been built up. As the Shemitah begins, the peaks of Wall Street begin to descend, to be brought low. And as the Shemitah reaches its last climactic day, the lines dramatically plummet.

On 9/11 Wall Street was shut down. It reopened on September 17, the Shemitah's climactic last day. Thus it was the first day that Wall Street bore the financial impact of 9/11. The greatest stock market point crash in history was the reflection of 9/11 in the financial realm. The two events were bound.

Even visually the crashing of the towers are mirrored in the plummeting of the graph down the side of a once colossal financial peak. The Shemitah wipes away what has been built up, whether the wealth of a nation's financial and economic realm or the physical towers that embody those realms.

So at the climax of the 2001 Shemitah came two falls—the most colossal stock market collapse in Wall Street history and the most colossal physical collapse in American history as the two towers came crumbling down to earth—the imploding and crashing of the financial realm, and the imploding and crashing in the physical realm, joined together in the "letting fall" of the Shemitah.

The Fall of Symbols

What had once stood on the pavement of Ground Zero were not only towers but colossal symbols of economic and financial power. The twin towers were, explicitly or implicitly, the most glaring and soaring icons of America's financial and economic prosperity, preeminence, and sovereignty. They epitomized the American-led global economic order that had prevailed since the end of the Second World War. On 9/11 that symbol came crashing down. If the World Trade Center was a symbol of America's economic and financial preeminence, then what would its collapse symbolize? Or can the fall of a symbol also be the symbol of a fall?

And what about the prophetic warning given to America at its inception and its connection to the nation's highest towers?

The towers had boasted of the nation's blessings and glory. But the warning reminded the nation that all its blessings and glory came from God. The towers epitomized the ascent and how far it had risen from its foundation. But the message warned that if America ever turned away from its foundation, its glory would not endure and the blessings of heaven would be removed from the land. In the fall of the soaring towers that had once epitomized the nation's blessings and glory, the words of the warning given in the days of its foundation now cried out from the ruins.

The Fall of Temples

In 586 BC the Shemitah fell upon the kingdom of Judah in the form of judgment. Second Chronicles records the most dramatic moment of that judgment:

> Then they burned the house of God, broke down the wall of Jerusalem, burned all its palaces with fire, and destroyed all its precious possessions.
> —2 Chronicles 36:19

The judgment involved an enemy attack. The enemy made a point of specifically attacking the nation's most prominent and majestic buildings. The chief of these was the nation's Temple, the edifice that represented the worship of its God. The buildings were set on fire and destroyed. The nation's holy ground was reduced to ruins.

When the Shemitah manifested in the form of judgment in September 2001, it too involved the attack of an enemy, an enemy who made a point of specifically focusing on America's most majestic buildings. The most prominent of these were the twin towers of the World Trade Center, two edifices symbolizing a god that the nation increasingly worshipped. The towers were set on fire and destroyed.

The Meaning of the Fall

We began the mystery of the towers with a solitary and unique edifice, a tower unlike any that had risen before it and that, in the year 1870, appeared on American soil. We saw the ancient link that joins together a nation's towers and its greatness, its magnitude, its rising, and its powers. We saw how the appearance of the tower of 1870 was joined to America's rise to world power. We now close the mystery in the smoldering ruins of two other towers. In their fall begins yet another mystery, that of the harbingers of judgment that appeared in the last days of ancient Israel, warning of judgment. With the fall of the towers they now appear to America bearing the same warning of coming judgment.

The question must now be asked: If the *rise* of a tower foreshadowed the rise of America in world history, what does the *fall* of a tower foreshadow?

———————

We now move to another realm to uncover one more dimension to the mystery of the Shemitah—one that concerns the rise and fall of nations.

PART VI

THE MYSTERY OF THE SHEMITAH AND THE RISE AND FALL OF NATIONS AND EMPIRES

Chapter 20

The RISING

The Shemitah of Kingdoms

Ｔʜᴇ Sʜᴇᴍɪᴛᴀʜ, ʙʏ nature, alters the scales. It changes the balance of accounts. Even on the smallest of scales it alters the balance of power. In its most far-reaching and prophetic manifestation the Shemitah's consequences are not limited to the financial and economic realms but extend into almost every realm of human existence and history. It can alter the landscape of nations, involve the rise and fall of great powers, and determine the fate of empires.

This can again be clearly seen in the events of 586 BC when the Shemitah, in the form of judgment, descends on the kingdom of Judah. It involves the political and military realms, the destruction of cities, the disappearance of a kingdom, and, on a larger scale, the rise and fall of empires.

Could the mystery of the Shemitah be at work affecting the rise and fall of nations in modern times?

The Time of Collapse

It is the Shemitah of September 1916 to September 1917. Did anything significant happen that year? We have already seen what happened in the financial realm. It would be known as the "Crisis of 1916–1917." It would rank as one of the top ten long-term collapses in stock market history, wiping out 40 percent of the market's value.

But what if we now go beyond the financial and economic realms? We have seen that behind the word *shemitah* is the verb "to shake." Was there any significant shaking at the time of that Shemitah?

There was—and it was perhaps the greatest shaking of nations in world history up to that moment. It was the time of the First World War. In it more than seventy million people served as military personnel. And more than fifteen million people died. It was unprecedented in scale, scope, and nature. The world had never seen anything like it.

The word *shemitah* is linked to the verb for "to let fall," "to cast down," and "to collapse." Was there a falling or collapse in the world at this time in world history, or associated with this war? Yes, but not just one. During the Shemitah there were, in process, four massive collapses of major world powers.

The Collapse of the German Empire

The German Empire, or Second Reich, was founded in 1871. In the time from its founding until the outbreak of the First World War, Germany had become one of the greatest powers on the world stage. It had boasted the world's most powerful army, the world's second most powerful navy, and the world's fastest-growing industrial base. But as a result of the First World War, the German Empire, the Second Reich, would collapse.

The Collapse of the Austro-Hungarian Empire

The Austro-Hungarian Empire was formed in 1867. It was one of the great powers on the world stage of the nineteenth and early twentieth centuries. But it was weakened by the fact that many of its different ethnic groups were seeking to have their own nation. As a result of the First World War the Austro-Hungarian Empire collapsed. Out of its ruins rose the nations of Czechoslovakia and Yugoslavia.

The Collapse of the Ottoman Empire

The Ottoman Empire had been a major player in world history for over six centuries. At its geographical high point, it controlled much of Western Asia, North Africa, Southeast Europe, the Horn of Africa, and the Caucasus. But as the armies of the Allied Powers advanced through the Middle East in the latter part of the First World War, the centuries-old empire began to collapse. Its collapse would bring about the creation of the Middle East as we now know it, including the emergence of the modern nation-states of Lebanon, Jordan, Saudi Arabia, and Israel, to name but a few.

The Collapse of the Russian Empire

The rule of the Russian czars had begun centuries before the First World War. The Russian Empire had been one of the largest empires in world history. In the nineteenth century its dominion reached from the Baltic Sea on the west to the Pacific Ocean on the east, and from the Black Sea on the south to the Arctic Ocean on the north. Only the British and Mongol empires had more land, and only China and the British Empire had more people.

But Russia's entrance into the First World War had resulted in severe military setbacks and economic disintegration. Discontent among soldiers and civilians alike reached crisis levels, and in the spring of 1917 revolution broke out in the city of Petrograd. Czar Nicholas abdicated the throne and the Russian Empire collapsed. In the autumn of 1917 the Bolsheviks, under the leadership of Vladimir Lenin, began the "October Revolution" and overthrew the Provisional Government. It was a watershed of history, the beginning of the first communist state, the birth of what would be called the "Soviet Union."

Each collapse was caused by the war, either by its process or its outcome. But for most of the war's duration, the outcome—and thus the majority of these collapses—was far from certain. What changed that? What proved to be the turning point?

1917: The Turning Point

From its earliest days as a nation America had sought to avoid entanglement in the affairs of other nations. With regard to global affairs, the nation had largely pursued a policy of nonintervention. It sought to maintain this policy in the face of the First World War. But in the spring of 1917, after a series of German submarine attacks on US merchant ships, America declared war on Germany.

The year 1917 is considered a turning point not only of the First World War but of world history. America's entrance into the war changed the balance of power and virtually ensured the defeat of the Central Powers and thus the collapse of empires.

The Shemitah year had begun on September 28, 1916, and concluded September 16, 1917. America entered World War I on April 6, 1917. Thus this pivotal event in American history and world history took place as part of the Shemitah. It would help bring about the collapse of three empires. The only collapse not affected by America's entrance was that of the Russian Empire. But the Russian Empire had collapsed in the same pivotal year, 1917, in the spring—and thus was part of the Shemitah year. In fact, these two pivotal events, the Russian Revolution and America's entrance into the First World War, not only both happened during the Shemitah, but they also happened within three weeks of each other.

The Nullification of Four Empires

Each one of the four collapses would dramatically alter the course of modern history. The collapse of the German and Austrian Empires would set the stage for the rise of Nazism and the Second World War. The collapse of the Ottoman Empire would set the stage for the conflicts of the Middle East. And the collapse of the Russian Empire would set the stage for the global spread of Communism and the Cold War. Each one of the four collapses was either brought about or ensured by the events of the Shemitah of 1917, or was itself one of those events.

The impact of the Shemitah is to bring nullification and the wiping away of that which has been built up. In its most global application this wiping away extends not only to economic and financial structures, but to physical structures and powers as well. By the end of the First World War the European landscape was filled with ruins. From the Western Front to the Eastern Front, from the Balkans to the Middle East, that which had been built up was wiped away. And on a larger scale, two empires that had taken decades to build up, and two others that had taken centuries, had now, likewise, been wiped away.

The Beginning of Sunset

But there was yet another collapse connected to the First World War and to the pivotal events of 1917. The greatest of all colonial powers was the British Empire. It had begun in the late sixteenth century. At its height, it had controlled almost one quarter of the world's land area, and one out of every five people on the planet lived under its dominion. Immediately after the war the empire reached its greatest geographical extent. It had been called "the empire on which the sun never sets." But the sun was about to set.

We have already seen the first sign of this decline at the time America built its first high tower and the title of "world's greatest economy" departs from the British Empire and moves to the New World. But as far as the decline of the empire itself, it is dated to the First World War. Going into the war, Britain had been the world's greatest creditor nation. But the war had decimated the British economy and consumed its national credit. The world's greatest creditor nation was now in debt. The financial disintegration would reach its peak in the war's latter part, when the empire approached near bankruptcy. When did that take place? It happened in 1917, the Year of the

Shemitah. After the war Britain would find itself increasingly unable to maintain its empire. The decline, at first, would be subtle, but by the century's midpoint it would turn into a full and ultimately total collapse.

The Rising Power

We have seen several falls linked to the Year of the Shemitah. But was there a rise? There was. While kingdoms and empires were falling, one was rising.

The First World War had drained the British Empire of financial and economic power, but it had the reverse effect on the United States. When the war broke out, America was a debtor nation. But when the war was over, America had not only ceased to be a debtor nation but had become the greatest creditor nation in the world. The British Empire, along with other world powers, was now heavily indebted to America.

The transference of mantles from the British Empire to America—a process that had begun in the late nineteenth century when America eclipsed Britain as the world's leading economic power—now entered its second phase. The financial and economic power departing from the British Empire on one hand was pouring into America on the other. The war had caused a massive transference of global power. The center of the world's financial realm had shifted from the Old World to the New, from the British Empire to the United States. The world's financial center was no longer London, but now New York City—the same city that now boasted the earth's highest towers.

Historians commonly mark the year 1917 as the beginning of America's rise to global superpower. It was the year that America ended its isolationism, and dramatically so. It was the key turning point, when the nation unequivocally walked onto the stage of world power. At the end of the war the shattered and exhausted powers of Europe now looked to America for leadership. America had taken on a mantle it was unprepared to assume. It was now not only the strongest economic power and the world's financial and economic center—it was now the leading nation on earth.

In the years following the war, America would seek to return to its former isolation—but there was no turning back. It had begun an irreversible rise to power that would take it to heights no nation or empire had ever known. And that ascent had begun in the Year of the Shemitah.

———————

The ascent of America to global superpower, having begun in the midst of one world war, would be completed at the end of the next. From America's entry into World War I to its emergence as global superpower in the ashes of World War II, the process would take twenty-eight years. Both 1917 and 1945 stand as key turning points in American and world history. They share, as well, another distinction: each is the Year of the Shemitah. America's rise to world superpower begins with one Shemitah and will be completed with another.

In 1945 the ancient mystery will manifest with such immensity of scale and force that the First World War will pale in comparison.

Chapter 21

The REIGNING

The Fourth Shemitah and
the Global Cataclysm

FOUR IS THE number given in Scripture connected to world kingdoms and empires. From the year America began its rise to superpower in the First World War to the coming of the Second World War, three Shemitahs had gone by. The fourth Shemitah was approaching. The world was again engaged in another cataclysm. It would be the deadliest war in human history. By the time it was over, more than fifty million lives would be lost.

The New World Order

The Year of the Shemitah would begin at summer's end 1944. In its approach American and Allied forces would launch the invasion of Europe, "Operation Overlord" on "D-Day." But in that same summer another event would take place, much more quietly, almost unnoticeably. And yet it would bear massive ramifications for the world. It would happen in the quiet village of Bretton Woods, New Hampshire.

The Shemitah brings about the transformation of the economic and financial realms. What took place at Bretton Woods would bring about the transformation of the global economic and financial order. It would establish such institutions as the World Bank and the International Monetary Fund. But most dramatically it would set up a new world economic and financial order in which world currencies would be tied to the US dollar.

The wiping away of debt and the ending of the Shemitah would bring about a new financial and economic beginning. Bretton Woods would bring about a new financial and economic beginning and order for the world. America would now be the global base on which the world's economic and financial order would rest. It was planned out in the summer of 1944, in the Shemitah's approach. It would be ratified by the American Congress in the Shemitah's midst, in summer of 1945. And it would begin taking effect after the war's end, in the Shemitah's wake.

But as the Shemitah also brings about collapse, so too Bretton Woods would do likewise. It heralded the end of the era of the British sterling's reign in world trade and the collapse of the British Empire. A senior official of the Bank of England described it as "the greatest blow to Britain next to the war."[1]

The Collapse of a Continent

The Shemitah began in September 1944 and lasted until September 1945. This period witnessed the war's most intense and climactic phase. The Year of the Shemitah had again brought the collapse of powers. As American and Allied forces marched across Europe from the west and the Red Army moved in from the east, the result was one of the most sweeping collapses of power in history. The totalitarian rule that had held an entire continent in an iron grip was overthrown. The Third Reich, which sought to destroy the children of Israel, had fallen in the Hebrew year of "the casting down."

Again the Shemitah changed the balance of nations. Again it ushered in a mass transference of power. Again it altered the landscape of history. And again there was a wiping away of what had been built up—a wiping away of governments, ideologies, armies, powers, buildings, states, cities, and sovereignties.

The Shemitah of World War II

World War II began when England and France declared war on Germany for invading Poland on September 1, 1939. But Hitler's seizure of Europe began a year earlier with the annexation of Austria in the spring of 1938, followed by the taking of the Sudetenland in Czechoslovakia in the autumn of 1938. Thus Hitler's takeover of nations began in 1938, the Year of the Shemitah. It would end with his suicide and the fall of the Third Reich in the spring of 1945, the following Year of the Shemitah. It had all taken place within the seven-year cycle, from Shemitah to Shemitah.

The Shemitah of the Holocaust

One can give a number of dates to mark the beginning of the Holocaust. But what is known as "The Fateful Year" was 1938. It was that year that the Nazi persecution of the Jews became an official and radicalized policy of the German state. On October 5, 1938, Jewish passports were invalidated. On October 27 came the brutal first mass deportation of Jewish people out of Germany. Two weeks later came *Kristallnacht*, "The Night of Broken Glass," when over fourteen hundred synagogues were set on fire, countless Jewish-owned shops and businesses were destroyed, and thirty thousand Jewish people were arrested and sent to concentration camps.

These events are commonly cited as the beginning of the Holocaust. It started in the month of Tishri, 1938, in the autumn wake of the Shemitah. The Holocaust would only end with the collapse of the Nazi state and the liberation of the death camps. Both would take place in the spring of 1945—in the Year of the Shemitah. It had all taken place in the seven-year cycle from Shemitah to Shemitah.

The Collapse of
the Colonial Empires

In 1945 one-third of the world lived in a territory under the dominion of or dependent on a colonial power. The same year marks the beginning of the fall of the great colonial empires. The war had devastated the European powers, the conquered and the conqueror alike. From the ruins of the Second World War began the collapse of the colonial empires. The rise of the two superpowers, America and the Soviet Union, would further accelerate that collapse. The fall of the European empires would affect every continent and give rise to multitudes of new nations. The Shemitah had now brought about one of the greatest series of collapses in history. Again, it had wiped away that which had been built up. And, again, it had altered the balance of powers and transformed the landscape of nations.

The Shemitah's End
and the Atomic Age

The war in Europe had ended in the spring of 1945, but the war against the Japanese Empire continued. It was still raging in the summer of 1945. As the Shemitah neared its climactic end, so did the Second World War. With one month left to the "end of the seventh year" and the time of nullification, the greatest destructive force ever devised by man was unleashed on the Japanese city of Hiroshima with the dropping of the atomic bomb. In a blinding flash the city was wiped away. Three days later another blinding flash would wipe away the city of Nagasaki.

At 12:00 noon, Japan standard time, August 15, the Emperor Hirohito announced the nation's surrender. The fall of the Japanese Empire would continue through the month of September with the surrender of troops from Burma to Hong Kong, from Korea to the islands of Miyako and Ishigaki. Thus the Empire's collapse and that of the war continued through the Hebrew month of Tishri in the Shemitah's autumn wake.

But the official end of the Second World War would come on September 2, 1945, aboard the USS *Missouri*, as the Japanese Empire issued its formal surrender to the Allies. The Second World War ended just as the Shemitah approached its end. In fact, the war would end in the Shemitah's last week, within days of Elul 29. The proximity of the end of the global conflict to the end of the ancient seven-year cycle was 99.99

percent. And at that same moment, at the Shemitah's peak, a new age would begin with America as the head of nations.

The Victor's Procession

The celebration of triumph at the end of war with a victorious procession of the prevailing army goes back to ancient times. At the end of the greatest war in world history there would be several such processions. In June of 1945 a Soviet victory parade was held by the Red Army in Moscow. In July the British forces held a victory parade in Berlin.

But few processions would involve all four of the Allied armies. And there would only be one that would mark the end of the Second World War at the actual time of the war's end. The procession took place in Berlin, the city in which the Third Reich fell and the war ended in Europe. It happened just days after the Japanese surrendered on the battleship USS *Missouri*, marking the end of the Second World War. Overseeing the victory parade was Marshal Georgy Zhukov, representing the Soviet Union; General George S. Patton, representing the United States; General Brian Robertson, representing the United Kingdom; and General Marie-Pierre Koenig, representing France.

It happened on September 7, 1945. But on the Hebrew calendar it was Elul 29, the day marking the end of the Shemitah—the very last day of the biblical cycle of seven years. The cycle had begun in 1938, the year in which Hitler's takeover of neighboring lands had begun and the fateful year that marked the beginning of the Holocaust. It had now ended seven years later on the last day of the Shemitah with the march of the victors through the streets of the conquered city. The procession marking the end of the greatest war in history took place on the very day appointed from ancient times to mark the end of the biblical cycle of seven years, on the Day of Remission, collapse, and release.

The Cold War Shemitah

But Elul 29 not only ends one cycle—but also its end begins another. The end of the war would mark the beginning of a new age, a new world, and a new conflict to be known as the Cold War.

From the same city in which the procession of Elul 29 took place, and from the same key players who took part in that procession, the Cold War would begin. Berlin would become the symbolic center of that conflict and that era, and of the division of that world between the two superpowers.

It has been noted by more than one commentator that what happened on that Day of the Shemitah in 1945 would become a point of contention between the two superpowers, a portent of the conflict that would become the Cold War. With the absence of General Eisenhower from the procession and the West's subsequent downplaying of the event, the day has been seen as the beginning of the end of the wartime coalition, one of the earliest signs of the ensuing global conflict, and a precursor of the Cold War—on the Day of the Shemitah.

The American Empire

Emerging from the ruins of the Second World War, America stood at a high pinnacle of world history. It was the greatest financial power, the greatest industrial power, the greatest commercial power, the greatest political power, the greatest military power, the greatest economic power, and the greatest cultural power on earth. The world's financial order, economic order, and political order were now led or driven by the American superpower. Its economy drove the world economy, its industry filled the world's markets, its culture filled the world's consciousness, and its military stood watch over the world's nations.

Some called it the "American Empire"; others, the "American Century"; and others, the "Pax Americana." Its rise had begun with the Shemitah of one world war and had now been sealed in the Shemitah of another. And it was just then, in the same year that had birthed the American superpower, that the idea of a World Trade Center was born.

But the Shemitah has two edges. To a nation that by and large upholds the ways of God, it comes as a blessing. But to a nation that has once known the ways of God but now rejects and defies them, the Shemitah comes not as a blessing but a judgment—and brings not a rising but a fall.

What happens if, from the pinnacle of 1945, we move forward the same span of time, another twenty-eight years, to the fourth Shemitah? Where will it bring us?

Chapter 22

The FALLING

The Fall

MOVING FORWARD THE same length of time as before, four periods of Shemitahs, twenty-eight years from America's zenith of power in 1945, we are brought to the year 1973. It is, of course, another Shemitah year. Unlike the first two cases, it wasn't marked by a world war. But was it significant? Very much so.

In the midst of its blessing, ancient Israel had begun driving God out of its government, out of its public squares, out of its culture, out of the instruction of its children. America had done likewise—beginning in the early 1960s as America banned prayer and the reading of Scripture from its public schools. The rulings were symptomatic of a larger removal of God from American culture. What followed was a decade of tumult and chaos. The nation was moving—slowly at first, and then with increasing speed—away from God and the ways of God.

The Blood of the Innocent

But 1973 would be a watershed in America's spiritual and moral descent. It was at the beginning of that year that the nation's highest court legalized the killing of unborn children. In the case of ancient Israel it was the killing of the nation's most innocent, its little children, that would ultimately lead to national judgment and destruction:

> And they rejected His statutes and His covenant that He had made with their fathers, and His testimonies which He had testified against them; they followed idols…So they left all the commandments of the LORD their God…And they caused their sons and daughters to pass through the fire…
> —2 KINGS 17:15–17

If the comparison seems severe, we must consider this: Israel killed thousands of its children; America has killed millions. At the time of this writing, the number of unborn children killed is estimated at over fifty million. If this was a cause for judgment concerning ancient Israel, a nation that had once known the ways of God but had now turned against them, then how could it be any less a cause for judgment concerning

America, a nation that had likewise once known the ways of God but had now turned against them?

The Long Decline

The Shemitah had begun in September 1972 and would continue until September 1973. The Supreme Court decision was issued in the midst of the Shemitah on January 22, 1973. The Shemitah can be linked to a nation's rise—or to its fall. The last two Shemitahs of this cycle—that of 1917 and 1945—were turning points concerning America's rising. But the Shemitah of 1973 was a turning point concerning its fall. It was the year America ruled it legal to kill its unborn children.

Only eleven days before that decision the stock market had reached its peak. In that same month it would change momentum and begin a long decline that would last into the autumn of 1974, having 48 percent of its worth wiped away. The collapse would then combine with a severe and crippling economic recession. It is worthy of note that the connection between the Year of the Shemitah and the collapses in America's financial and economic realms appears to grow more intense and consistent in the cycles immediately following the critical year of 1973 than in those preceding it.

The Collapse of Bretton Woods

The Bretton Woods system, established at the end of World War II in 1945, was based on tying the world's major currencies to the US dollar and the US dollar being tied to the gold standard. But by the 1960s America did not have enough gold to back up its dollars. The dollar had weakened. In August 1971 President Nixon removed the US dollar from the gold standard. And in the spring of 1973 the bonds tying the world's currencies to the dollar were irrevocably severed. Bretton Woods, which, at the end of the Second World War, had epitomized America's hegemony over the world's financial and economic order, had collapsed.

Bretton Woods was joined to the Shemitah in its beginning. So it would be joined to the Shemitah in its end. Again, the Shemitah had brought about a collapse. And again, it had touched the world's economic and financial realms.

"Before Your Enemies"

As America turned from God, over the long term its position relative to the rest of the world continued to deteriorate. The Bible cites several signs of God's favor on a nation. One of these is economic prosperity. Another is military power and victory. At the end of the Second World War America stood at the pinnacle of both economic and military power. But now its "almighty dollar" was weakening, and a series of crises was causing a deterioration in its economic power. What about its military power?

As the nation began driving God out of its life in the 1960s, its military fortunes began to change. The change had a name: Vietnam. For the first time in over a century and a half—some would say for the first time *ever*—America had lost a war. What year did America lose its first war in modern times? It happened in 1973, the Year of the Shemitah. America's greatest military victory had taken place in the Year of the Shemitah. So too now did its most traumatic military defeat.

Four Shemitahs, twenty-eight years, earlier America had won the Second World War, its greatest military victory. That day was August 15, 1945. So America's first military defeat in modern history took place on the anniversary of its greatest military victory—a sign concerning the removal of God's blessing—and yet another manifestation of collapse in the Year of the Shemitah.

The Cycles of the Fourth Shemitah

Behind the rising and falling of America is a mystery of Shemitahs. The key turning points of that rise and fall were each connected to the Shemitah year. Each of these turning points took place during the fourth Shemitah from the last turning point—intervals of twenty-eight years.

- **The cycle of superpower**—America's rise to world power begins in the Year of the Shemitah 1917 with its entrance into the First World War. Moving forward twenty-eight years, we come to the fourth Shemitah in the year 1945. In 1945 America's rise to world superpower is completed.

- **The cycle of Bretton Woods**—At its pinnacle of power America becomes the center of a new world financial and economic order, the Bretton Woods system, at the time of the Shemitah 1945. Moving forward twenty-eight years, we come to the fourth Shemitah in the year 1973—the year that the Bretton Woods system undergoes its final collapse. It begins and ends with the Shemitah.

- **The cycle of war**—On August 15, 1945, the empire of Japan surrenders. The Second World War is over. Having won its greatest military victory in history, America stands at the pinnacle of military power. Moving forward twenty-eight years, we come to the fourth Shemitah, in the year

1973—the year America ends its war in Vietnam
in defeat—its first military loss in modern history.
The defeat comes on August 15, 1973, twenty-
eight years after its greatest victory—to the day.

The Cycle of the Tower

But there was one more connection in the mystery. At America's apex of global power an idea was born that would parallel that apex. America, the now undisputed center of world
trade, would build a World Trade Center. The building would
embody the new American-led financial and economic world
order. After many delays and obstacles the vision of 1945
would finally become a reality. The year was 1973. It had been
conceived in the Shemitah, and in the Shemitah it would be
finished. From the conception to the completion was, again,
twenty-eight years, and, again, it was the fourth Shemitah.

The Testament and the Fall

What happened in America in 1973 was as critical as that
which happened in 1917 and 1945. The ramifications of a
nation, founded and blessed by God, so dramatically turning
against the Word of God in making legal the killing of its
unborn children, are immense. For a similar sin of violence
against its children, an ancient nation was brought into judgment and destroyed.

It was the same year in which America legalized the killing
of its unborn that the nation would suffer its first military
defeat in modern history. That same year would begin a long-
term financial collapse that would combine with one of the
most severe economic recessions in its history. And that same
year the global economic order that had been founded with
America as its pillar suffered its final collapse.

And then there were the towers, conceived in America's crowning moment, to stand as monuments of the nation's new global supremacy. But they did not stand at the time of America's pinnacle but twenty-eight years later in 1973, a turning point of a very different nature.

It was the year of the soaring towers that testified of the nation's ascendancy. But it was also the year that America began legally killing its unborn children. The World Trade Center was a symbol, on one hand, of a nation's ascending and, on the other, of its moral and spiritual descent. It was a monument to a nation's glory on one hand and a testament to its sin and shame on the other. It was a memorial of a nation's fall, marking the year America began killing its most defenseless. The towers would bear witness of two glaringly different realities, each in deep conflict with the other. And the days of their coexistence would be numbered.

The Last Cycle

What happens now if we move forward one last cycle, twenty-eight years, to the fourth Shemitah? Where will it bring us?

It will bring us to 2001—to the Shemitah of 9/11—in which the monument to America's ascendant glory and unmatched powers would be destroyed. The testament of the American-led world order would be cast down. In 2001 the cycles that had begun in 1945 would come full circle:

- The towers had been conceived in the Shemitah of 1945 at America's apogee. On the fourth Shemitah, twenty-eight years later in 1973, they were completed. For twenty-eight years they stood. On the fourth Shemitah after their completion, in the year 2001, they were destroyed.

- In the Shemitah of 1945 America had defeated all of its enemies and emerged from the ruins of other nations victorious and unrivaled in military power. On the fourth Shemitah, twenty-eight years later, it suffered its first military defeat in modern history, on enemy soil, in 1973, on the same date of its apogee. Twenty-eight years after that, on the fourth Shemitah, in 2001, the enemy would come to America, and the nation would suffer destruction on its own soil.

- In the Shemitah of 1945 a new world order based on American economic and financial power was inaugurated. On the fourth Shemitah, twenty-eight years later in 1973, that order would suffer collapse. Twenty-eight years after that, on the fourth Shemitah, in 2001, the symbol of the American-led global economy would also collapse.

The same Shemitah that brings collapse to one power, nation, or kingdom may bring the rise of another. As far as America is concerned, for much of its history and over the long-term, it had appeared to be largely on the rising side of this equation. But in recent times it has appeared to be much more on the falling side—paralleling its moral and spiritual fall from God.

What lies ahead? What does the future hold for America and the nations? And what might the mystery of the Shemitah reveal about that future? To these questions we now turn.

PART VII

THE MYSTERY OF THE SHEMITAH AND THAT WHICH LIES AHEAD

Chapter 23

The LAST TOWER

The Other Tower

THE DESTRUCTION OF the twin towers was not the end in the mystery of the towers. There would be another. It would rise up from the site on which the twin towers had been stuck down—Ground Zero. It would become a symbol of the rebuilding of America in the wake of 9/11. American leaders would speak of it even before it came into existence and then, as it rose, hail its rising as a symbol of the nation's

pride and resilience. The tower would stand as the embodiment of America itself.

And yet behind its rising lay an ancient mystery.

The Defiant Ascent

In the face of the enemy attack that involved the destruction
of buildings and the first warning of national judgment—the
people of Israel responded with defiance. They issued their
fateful vow:

> The bricks have fallen down, but we will rebuild with
> hewn stones...
> —ISAIAH 9:10

They would defy the warning given them. They would
rebuild that which had collapsed into ruins on the day of terror.
The rebuilding would be an act of defiance. They would rebuild
their fallen buildings bigger, stronger, better, and higher than
before. It wasn't the rebuilding that was wrong, but the intent
behind it. They would not listen to God's warning but would
defy it. And that which they would erect would stand as a
monument, not of their resurgence, but of their defiance—a
defiance that would ultimately lead to their destruction.

The Defiant Rising Revisited

In the wake of 9/11, America's leaders responded, as did those
of ancient Israel—not with repentance, but with defiance. Soon
after the attack they began vowing to rebuild what had been
struck down and to build it bigger and stronger than before.
More than one spoke of the rebuilding of Ground Zero as an
act of defiance. The nation would not be humbled or repent,
but it would vow to rise again stronger than before.

The Hebrew Tower

But where does a tower come in? The ancient vow in Isaiah makes no mention of what exactly is to be rebuilt. The vow does speak of rebuilding what had fallen. This must have involved buildings and, in view of ancient warfare, would have involved towers. But we have another clue. The Hebrew behind Isaiah's prophecy, as we have seen, carries deeper meaning than the English translation conveys. We have seen this in the verse that introduces the ancient vow:

> *Who say in pride and arrogance of heart:* "The bricks have fallen down, but we will rebuild with hewn stones..."
>
> —ISAIAH 9:9–10,
> *EMPHASIS ADDED*

The vow is spoken in pride and arrogance. The Hebrew word for "arrogance," as we have seen, is *gadal*, which is linked to the word for "tower." So we have a Hebrew word meaning "rebuild" and another linked to the word *tower*. The rebuilding would embody the nation's defiant pride—and no structure better embodies pride than a tower.

The Greek Tower

The earliest translation ever made of the Bible is called the *Septuagint*. The Septuagint is the translation of the Hebrew Scriptures into Greek. It is this translation that is extensively quoted in the New Testament. When the Septuagint comes to Isaiah 9:10, something striking happens:

> The bricks are fallen down, but come...and let us build for ourselves a *tower*."

The ancient translation specifically speaks of the building of a tower. In other words, after the attack, on the same ground on which the bricks had fallen, there would rise a tower.

And that is exactly what happened in America. At Ground Zero, where the nation had been attacked, where the bricks had fallen, a tower began to rise.

The Tower of Defiance

Even before the tower existed, it had been spoken of by American leaders. One of the nine prophetic signs of judgment recorded in *The Harbinger* is called "The Prophecy." It manifested on the day after 9/11 when the United States Congress gathered on Capitol Hill to issue America's response to the calamity. There, from the floor of the House of Representatives, the vow of defiance that brought judgment and destruction to ancient Israel was now proclaimed in America.

In that prophetic moment an American leader vowed that the nation would rebuild that which had fallen. Implicit in those words was the rebuilding of the World Trade Center. This was the first official proclamation of the rebuilding. Thus the tower at Ground Zero was actually *brought into existence* with the ancient words of Israel's judgment, through *the ancient words of Isaiah 9:10.*

This would be followed by more declarations issued by other American leaders, each one echoing another aspect of the ancient vow. One declared that the tower had to be built to show the world that America was defiant. Another charged that the tower had to be built higher than the towers it replaced—bigger, taller, and greater.

The tower would be more than a building; it would be the most colossal American symbol ever constructed. At a planned height of 1,776 feet, a number chosen to mirror America's year of independence, it was clear that the tower was a representation of the nation itself, rising up from the ruins, proud, unbowed, and defiant. But as much as it was an embodiment of America, it was also an embodiment of the ancient vow of judgment in Isaiah 9:10.

The Spirit of Babel

From where did the ancient Jewish scholars of the Septuagint get the phrase "Come...let us build for ourselves a tower" to use as the translation of Isaiah 9:10? They got it from Genesis 11, from the account of the Tower of Babel.

> And they said, "*Come, let us build ourselves* a city, and *a tower* whose top is in the heavens; let us make a name for ourselves..."
>
> —Genesis 11:4,
> *EMPHASIS ADDED*

Why did the translators use the words of Babel to translate Isaiah 9:10 in the first place? It was because they saw a direct connection between the building project of Genesis 11 and that of Isaiah 9:10. Both were based on pride and arrogance. Both were executed in defiance of God.

So, now, America too embarked on the building of a tower at Ground Zero. It would first be known as the "Freedom Tower" and then "One World Trade Center." The tower was conceived and executed in the spirit of pride and defiance. It had even been planned from the outset that the new tower would become the tallest building on the earth. But before it could be completed, other towers had ascended to greater heights. But the spirit of Babel infused the project from the beginning.

The Shemitah and the Last Tower

We have earlier seen that the mystery of the Shemitah and the mystery of the towers converge. What about the rising tower at Ground Zero? Is there anything linking it to the mystery of the Shemitah? There is.

First is its origin. It replaced the World Trade Center, which, as we have seen, was conceived, started, finished, and destroyed in the Year of the Shemitah. That building, in turn, had replaced, as the world's tallest building, the Empire State Building, which, in turn, had been completed in the Year of the Shemitah.

When and where was the tower of Ground Zero conceived? The tower was publicly conceived the day after 9/11 on Capitol Hill, when the ancient vow was spoken and it was proclaimed that America would rebuild that which had been destroyed. The proclamation took place on September 12, 2001, in the last days of the Shemitah. Thus, even by a matter of days, the tower of defiance was conceived in the Year of the Shemitah.

The construction of the new tower would be mired in controversy, obstructions, and setbacks. It would take years before the building actually began. At the end of 2006 the ground was cleared to begin the foundation. In 2007 came the preparing of the foundation. At the beginning of 2008 the building's core began rising, ultimately to reach street level. The Shemitah was 2007–2008. Though the foundation and preparatory work began earlier, the rising of the tower began in the Year of the Shemitah.

Omens

In the spring of 2012 the tower had finally surpassed the height of the Empire State Building to become the tallest building in the New York skyline. The date on which it happened had already appeared in *The Harbinger* four months before it occurred. It was the date linked to the mystery of Ground Zero.

In the summer of 2012, six months after *The Harbinger*'s release, the president of the United States made a visit to Ground Zero. There he took part in a ceremony that comprised an ominous prophetic act in accordance with the mystery. It was one of the continuing manifestations of *The Harbinger* mentioned earlier. He would unwittingly seal the connection between the tower and the ancient vow, a connection foretelling the coming of judgment.

At the president's second inauguration in January 2013, the chosen poet laureate recited a poem to the thousands gathered and the millions watching by television. In it he spoke of giving thanks, not to God, but to "the work of our hands."[1] Then as part of "the work of our hands," he spoke of the future completion of the tower at Ground Zero:

> ...the last floor on the Freedom Tower
> Jutting into a sky
> That yields to our resilience...[2]

It is nearly impossible not to hear in those words the echoing of the ancient vow of Isaiah 9:10—a nation praising its own powers, placing its trust in the works of its hands, its building of an edifice to defiantly jut into the sky, a tower to make the heavens yield in the face of its collective resilience. It was hard as well not to hear the echo of Babel.

Less than four months later the giant spire was placed on the tower's pinnacle, to complete its height. In the rabbinical writings it is said that a solar eclipse is a sign of judgment upon the nations. It is not known from where the idea comes, if not derived from the scriptural references to the darkening of the sun on the Day of Judgment. But as something to note, the day they set the spire on top of the tower the sun was darkened. The tower reached its highest elevation on the day of a solar eclipse.

At the time of this writing, the tower still awaits its completion.

The Towering Harbinger

If the tower at Ground Zero is a harbinger, what is it a harbinger of? Of what does it portend?

The rising of America's high towers have marked and paralleled America's rising to the heights of world power and prosperity. But if the rising of a tower can bear witness of the rising of a nation, then of what does the fall of a tower bear witness? The unavoidable answer is this: it bears witness of the fall of a nation.

The same nation that was once marked by the rise of the world's highest towers is no longer marked by them. It is now marked by their falling. And it has all taken place at the same time in that nation's history, when the signs grow increasingly evident of the decline of its powers. And even more telling, it has all taken place when the signs of that nation's spiritual and moral descent have grown overwhelmingly stark.

Towers, by nature, carry symbolic meaning. But rarely has a tower been vested with so much symbolic meaning as that which rose from the pavement of Ground Zero. But beyond any meaning assigned to it by its builders, the tower's significance is prophetic. In this case the nation's foremost tower is not simply a tower—but a harbinger—the fourth harbinger in an ancient biblical template of judgment. It speaks of a nation attempting to scale the heavens while, at the same time, descending from God—a physical rising and a spiritual fall—two conflicting realities.

The rising tower at Ground Zero was not only birthed by the ancient vow of Isaiah 9:10, but it is also its embodiment. The tower is the vow in concrete. It shouts of defiance. It tells of a nation that had once known God but then, in its blessings, turned against Him and warred against His ways. And it testifies of a people warned, shaken, and called by God to return, but who ignore the warning, who reject the call, and who attempt to beat back the effects of that shaking and rise higher than before, by virtue of their own powers, and against the ways of God.

Can such a nation again ascend to its former heights of glory while, at the same time, warring against the God of its foundation? The case of ancient Israel is a warning against such a nation's attempt to rebuild itself stronger than before. For the tower it builds, as it was with the first tower ever recorded in Scripture, will be a harbinger of coming judgment.

Chapter 24

THAT WHICH LIES AHEAD

The Eyes of the Prophet

THE PROPHET GAZED into the smoldering ruins of the holy
city. He had been given warning by God and had, in turn,
given warning to his nation. But they didn't listen. They cast
him into prison and continued on their course of defiance
until the judgment finally came.

The year 586 BC was one of history's turning points. Jeremiah was there to see it firsthand just as he was there to foretell

it. As he now beheld the desolation of the holy city, he could not
escape grappling with a mystery begun many centuries earlier
in the wilderness of Sinai. The Law of Moses had foretold the
day of destruction. According to the ancient words, the people
would be sent into exile and the land would rest. And the time
of that rest and desolation would be determined by the number
of Sabbath years, the Shemitahs, the nation had broken.

As he surveyed the city of God now lying still and silent—
desolate and devoid of its inhabitants—the prophet wept and
pondered the mystery of the covenant. He knew that the word
shemitah meant "the release." And now the land had been
released. He knew also that it signified "the letting fall." And
now God had allowed the holy city to fall and the kingdom of
Judah itself to collapse. The prophet could now only wonder
how the ancient mystery of the Shemitah could have so determined the fate of his nation.

The Mystery of the Shemitah

We now stand two and a half thousand years later, pondering
the same mystery as pondered by the prophet in the ruins. We
also may wonder how such an ancient mystery has so determined the course of nations, world markets, empires, and
history. And as the prophet saw the mystery become flesh-
and-blood reality in his own life and time when the cataclysm
fell upon the land, it is now for us as well to bring the mystery
home to our day and age, to see what it may hold and reveal
concerning the future of America and the world.

We have seen an ancient ordinance of Scripture concerning
a seventh year of rest and a Day of Remission transform into
a mystery. We have observed the mystery growing larger in
scope and dimensions to the point of involving the destruction of an ancient city and the exile of its people to a foreign

land. We have moved forward in time to find the same mystery spanning thousands of years and operating in the modern world. We have witnessed its dynamics at work in the financial and economic realms, determining the rising and crashing of world markets, the economies of modern nations, and the greatest collapses in financial history. We have seen it coalesce with a mystery of towers, again joined to the dynamics of rising and falling. And we have watched it move on the stage of world history, determining the rise and fall of nations, the ascendancy of world powers and the collapse of empires.

The Quickening

What about the future? And why might the mystery of the Shemitah be especially relevant to our day and the days to come?

In the last two of the Shemitah's cycles, those ending in 2001 and 2008, we have noticed a number of significant developments. First, the timing has become amazingly precise. Both of the last two greatest stock market point crashes in history have occurred on the exact same Hebrew day and the Shemitah's exact same climactic Day of Remission and Nullification. The phenomenon appears, in its last manifestations, to have grown increasingly precise and dramatic.

Second, the phenomenon of the last two cycles was begun and triggered by one of the most dramatic events of modern times: 9/11. If it were not for 9/11, the ancient mystery would not have manifested. If it were not for the exact timing of 9/11, the timing of the stock market crash of 2001 would not have happened when it did at the time and in the exact hours of the Shemitah's climactic conclusion.

Third, the amazing precision of the Shemitah's last two occurrences are connected to the manifestation of harbingers, prophetic signs concerning the judgment of a nation—namely,

America. Combine this with the fact that the Shemitah, in Scripture, manifests as a sign of national judgment—and we have a convergence of alarms.

Since we are dealing with the issue of judgment, our first question must be this: What has happened to America in the time of these last two cycles in which the phenomenon has intensified?

The Deepening

Though in the wake of 9/11 Americans gathered in houses of worship across the land and it appeared as if there would be a national return to God—it never came. In place of the revival was a spiritual and moral apostasy that was unprecedented in its scope and accelerating pace. There was now increasing talk concerning the end of "Christian America." Polls noticed a growing departure from biblical ethics and values. The turn was most pronounced among the younger generation, portending a future of even greater moral and spiritual departure.

In the fall of ancient Israel the nation decided it could rewrite morality and change what was good and evil, sin and righteousness—so too in America. What had once been recognized as right was now attacked as evil, and what had once been recognized as sin was now celebrated as a virtue. Morals, standards, and values that had undergirded not only the nation's foundation, but also the foundation of Western civilization and civilization itself, were increasingly overturned, overruled, and discarded. And those who would not go along with the change— who merely continued to uphold that which had once been universally upheld—were now increasingly marginalized, vilified, condemned by the culture and the state, and persecuted.

And not only did the blood of unborn children continue to flow, as it did in ancient Israel, but the number of those killed was now well over fifty million, a population of many Israels.

The nation's moral descent had now reached the point where the government was seeking to force those who held to God's Word to go against that Word, punishing resistance with fines, damages, and condemnation. Any deviation from the new ethics of apostasy was swiftly punished. At the same time, the name of God increasingly became the object of attack, mockery, and blasphemy.

The Dark City on the Hill

It seemed as if every day a new threshold of apostasy and moral descent had been crossed. America was in moral and spiritual collapse and rapidly transforming into the dark opposite of the "city on a hill," the "holy commonwealth" it had been founded to be. It had now entered the territory of ancient Israel's apostasy—a nation to which the prophets cried out:

> Woe to those who call evil good, and good evil; who put darkness for light, and light for darkness.
> —Isaiah 5:20

And that was the point. America, having been formed after the pattern of ancient Israel, was now following in the course of Israel's apostasy. Thus it could be no accident that the same harbingers that appeared in the last days of ancient Israel were now reappearing in America. And each of those harbingers was warning of a coming judgment. Worse than that, America was responding to those warnings with the same defiance as had ancient Israel before judgment fell.

The Tipping Point

If one begins to tip over an object, a clear point is reached when one no longer needs to expend more energy or effort.

The object is on the edge, and the slightest push will send it over. The edge of its falling is the tipping point. Once the tipping point is reached, the object will fall by itself with accelerating force. When a tipping point is reached, the dynamics change. Things accelerate. So it is with a nation.

It was at a critical tipping point in America's descent from biblical morality that *The Harbinger* was released. Before God brings judgment, He warns. Since that time, the nation's apostasy from the ways of God has not lessened but has dramatically accelerated.

The Harbingers Unstopped

The Harbinger reveals the replaying of an ancient mystery of national judgment in twenty-first-century America. The mystery involves specific signs of warning given to ancient Israel in its last days now manifesting in America. That would be enough. But the mystery has not stopped. Since the release of the book, the mystery has continued. The harbingers have continued to manifest. And that which was written or foreshadowed in the book has been coming true. What does it mean?

The continuation of the harbingers signifies that the nation's defiance of God has likewise continued. In other words, the progression of the harbingers reflects the progression of the apostasy—and thus the nation's advance to judgment.

To Whom Much Is Given

The mystery presented in *The Harbinger* leads to an unavoidable question:

> If America has followed in the same apostasy of ancient
> Israel, witnessed the manifesting of the same harbingers of
> judgment that appeared in ancient Israel, and responded

to the warnings given with the same defiance with which
ancient Israel responded, how then can it escape suffering
the same judgment suffered by ancient Israel?

Some would object that other nations have exceeded
America in all of these sins. But so it was in the ancient world.
There was no shortage of examples of other nations that had
exceeded Israel in all of the sins for which its judgment would
come. But there was a major difference. God had revealed
Himself to Israel. He had sent to the nation His Word, given
them His law, revealed to them His ways. And He had blessed
them with peace, prosperity, and protection.

It is written, "To whom much is given, from him much will
be required" (Luke 12:48). Israel was given much. And much
was required. The standards were higher and the judgment,
when it came, more severe. So too has America been given
much. The Word of God has filled its culture, and the blessings of God have filled its land. No nation in the modern world
has been given so much blessing. But to whom much is given,
much is required. If America has been given much, then much
will be required. And its sins must be severely judged.

The Judgment Pattern

Going by the template of the ancient judgment revealed in *The
Harbinger*, a clear pattern emerges. First come warnings through
voices, the voice of God in the voices of the righteous, or the
faithful, or the prophets. But with these first warnings going
unheeded, there now comes warning in less gentle manifestations. God allows the nation to be shaken. It is still the calling
of God, but to a people who have now grown so hardened and
deafened to His voice that it is only in this way that they can

hear—if they will hear. It is a wake-up call and a warning that if the nation does not return to God, judgment will come.

If, after the first calamity or shaking, the nation still does not hear or respond, there comes a second shaking. And if the nation still does not hear, or still ignores, or still rejects the warning in the second shaking, there comes another, and another, until the nation either turns back to God and is restored, or continues down its course to the full force of the judgment. And there is no guarantee as to how many warnings or shakings are given before that judgment falls.

When Judgment Comes

And as for that judgment, how does it come? A nation's judgment can come through another nation or nations. It can come through natural disaster. It can come through unnatural or man-made disaster. It can come through a second strike on the land, or a second manifestation of terrorism. It can come through economic and financial collapse. It can come through famine. It can come through the breakdown of infrastructure. It can come through military defeat. It can come through decline, disorder, division, and disintegration. There is no formula for it, but there are patterns and templates of its progression.

The Harbinger Prophecies

The nine harbingers of ancient Israel were not merely events or objects, but prophetic signs. And as prophetic signs, they each carried prophetic messages concerning not only the nation's present condition—but also that which lay ahead in its future, prophecies in the form of signs revealing what would happen if the nation didn't turn back to God.

Since the same nine harbingers have now manifested in America, is it possible that the prophetic messages they carried concerning ancient Israel's future could also reveal what could lie ahead in America's future? In the space we have here, we will just briefly touch on two of the prophetic warnings contained in the nine harbingers.

The Oracle of the Breach

The breaking of Israel's hedge of national security in 732 BC was not just a calamity but a prophetic warning of things to come. The warning was this:

If the nation did not return to God and continued to war against His ways, a strike of a much greater scale and fury would come upon the land—and the nation would be destroyed.

And that is exactly what would happen on Israel's last day as a nation. The breach was a harbinger of things to come. It had been carried out by Assyrian soldiers. So too, years later, the nations' final destruction would be carried about by the Assyrians. The first strike was a foreshadowing of the last.

What about America? The breach of America's security manifested in 9/11. But if 9/11 was not just a calamity but a prophetic foreshadower, what is its warning? According to the ancient pattern, the warning would be this:

Without God, there is no true security or safety for America. Without His hand of protection, no matter how many systems of defense the nation employs, they will fail just as they did on 9/11. America cannot defy the God of its keeping and expect that protection to continue. "Unless the LORD guards the city, the watchman stays awake in vain" (Ps. 127:1). America, without God, is not safe. America, in defiance of God, is even less safe. If it continues down the present course, another calamity may come on the land as on 9/11, and yet on an even greater scale.

The Oracle of the Ruins

After the strike on ancient Israel in 732 BC, all that was left of the buildings that had stood in the path of the enemy's onslaught were the ruin heaps of fallen bricks—the third harbinger. The bricks were not just the remnants of destruction, but also foreshadowings of what was yet to come. They were prophecies in ruin heaps. Their warning was twofold. The first was this:

- If the nation continued in its course, a greater destruction would befall it, and the ruin heaps of fallen bricks that appeared in limited number and scale, the result of a limited strike, would become nearly universal. The ruins would appear throughout the land. The nation itself would be left in ruins.

The second warning of the fallen bricks was larger:

- The fallen bricks spoke of collapse, implosion, a crumbling, the wiping away of structure, disintegration, and destruction. The second warning was this: if the people didn't heed the warning, the kingdom itself would crumble, collapse, implode, be destroyed. And that is exactly what would take place in the years that followed. The kingdom of Israel would be wiped away from the land.

The third harbinger manifested in America in the fall of the towers and the massive ruin heaps that appeared at Ground Zero in their place. According to the pattern of Israel's judgment, the warning would be this:

- America cannot war against the God of its foundation and expect its blessings to remain. If
America does not turn from its course, it will
become vulnerable to a future event of even
greater destruction.

And beyond this is a larger warning. The bricks, the ruin
heaps, and 9/11 itself speak of collapse, implosion, disintegration, and destruction. The larger warning would be this:

- In His blessings God allowed America to be built
up, as a high tower among the nations. But a
tower cannot separate itself from the very foundation on which it rests and still stand. So too
with America—without God America will not
hold but will collapse.

What adds to the message is that the towers that fell on 9/11
carried specific symbolic meaning. They represented America's
financial and economic power and preeminence. In their collapse the warning of the bricks would speak of economic and
financial implosion. We have already seen manifestations of
this in the two great collapses of Wall Street in the Shemitahs
of 2001 and 2008.

Lastly, the towers represented a global financial and economic order and age in which America was the center. Even
the name World Trade Center conveys this. What of their fall?
It would warn of coming days when America is no longer the
center of the world's financial and economic order—and when
that order itself has collapsed.

Isaiah 9:11 and Beyond

Beyond the prophetic keys contained in the other seven harbingers concerning America are the keys contained in the prophecy itself. If one reads beyond the vow of defiance in Isaiah 9:10, starting with verse 11, one finds an account of national judgement—the specific judgments that came upon ancient Israel in the years after the harbingers appeared. The description is chilling in its unrelenting execution.

Though we would not expect the unique circumstances surrounding Israel's destruction to constitute a formula for the present, there are some striking things to note. The scenario concerns:

- Ungodly leaders
- A government passing immoral laws
- Division
- Violence
- A desolation that comes from far away
- An enemy attack
- Fire on the land
- Destruction

The Shemitah and the Mystery of the Future

What about the harbinger of the Shemitah? Could its mystery reveal that which lies ahead?

As I wrote at the beginning of this book, we must be careful with regard to date-setting as to when certain events must come about. The issue is not of dates but of the call to repentance and return. My concern with the focusing on dates is that it can take away from the central matter of repentance. I have warned of a coming judgment, but I have also cautioned against putting the workings of God in a box with regard to the timing of that judgment. God doesn't *have* to act in the same way or according to the same timing as He has in the past. Prophetic signs do not generally happen routinely or according to a schedule. There are Shemitah years that dramatically manifest the mystery and others that do not. Nothing *has to* happen in the next Shemitah.

Having said that, I must also give a second caution: God *can* work as He has in the past and *can* bring judgment at the time of the Shemitah. In view of both cautions, it is wise that one should be aware of the Shemitah and its days.

The Opening and Closing Pattern

While nothing of significance has to take place in any given Shemitah year, if something of significance were to happen, how might it manifest? The Shemitah's opening can mark the beginning of change and the shifting of momentum. At the same time, if a change or shifting should take place at this point, more often than not it tends to constitute a firstfruit, a foreshadow of what lies ahead, a subtle trace in comparison to what comes at the end. If there is a change at this point, its coming may or may not be noticeable at first.

The general pattern is this: As the Shemitah progresses, and, particularly, as it nears its end, its intensity increases. As the Shemitah approaches the time of its climactic day and wake, it is then that the dramatic events associated with its coming either manifest, intensify, or approach their climax.

In the case of September 2000, the Shemitah's beginning paralleled a downturn in national production, one of the signs of recession. But one could easily have missed it. Halfway through the Shemitah, the downturn coalesced into a full recession. And yet the Shemitah's most dramatic moment manifested in its last week. It was the week that the attack of 9/11 and the subsequent collapse of Wall Street took place. The overall pattern is that the Shemitah's most dramatic or intense time is that which leads up to Elul 29 or that which proceeds from Elul 29, the Day of Nullification.

The Shemitah to Come

So when is the next Shemitah? The Shemitah begins in September of 2014. Its first day, Tishri 1, commences at sunset on Wednesday night, September 24, and ends at sunset on September 25. But again, it is at the Shemitah's end and its wake that the most dramatic repercussions are felt. In each of the last two Shemitahs the end date of Elul 29 saw the greatest collapses in stock market history. The coming Shemitah will end September 2015. Its final climactic day, Elul 29, the Day of Remission, will fall on Sunday, September 13. Since the stock markets are closed, this would preclude the beginning of a market collapse that day, inasmuch as America is concerned.

But there are other possibilities. While nothing has to take place on or around this time, if something were to happen, a collapse or calamity could take place just before or after that weekend, or both before and after. It could also take place within the larger Elul-Tishri period surrounding Elul 29. Another possibility is that of a trigger event that takes place outside the time of the markets' openings that could bring about a market collapse—as in the case of 9/11. And there is the possibility of a calamity taking place beyond and apart from the financial and economic realms, and yet which causes the collapse of both these realms.

It is worthy to note that as it was in 2001, so it will be again in 2015—the last day the market will be open before Elul 29, the Day of Nullification, will be September 11.

During 2015 there will be two solar eclipses. Interestingly both of them will bear significance with regard to the Shemitah's timing. One will mark the Shemitah's exact center point. The other will mark its climactic last day, Elul 29. The last time a solar eclipse fell on Elul 29 of a Shemitah year was twenty-eight years earlier in September 1987. It ushered in the greatest stock market percentage crash in American history that same month. (See the epilogue for more about these solar eclipses as well as blood moons.)

The What of the Mystery

Again, as stated before, we cannot expect prophetic happenings to show up on a regular schedule or to perform on cue. Nothing significant *has* to happen within the Shemitah of 2014–2015. The phenomenon may manifest in one cycle, and not in another, and then again in the next. And the focus of the message is not date-setting but the call of God to repentance and return. At the same time, something of significance could take place, and it is wise to note the times.

Regardless of what does or does not take place in the coming Shemitah, and regardless of the *when* involved in the mystery, it is wise that we now take note of the *what*—the mystery's essence—and apply it to America and the world concerning a judgment in days to come.

The Mystery of the Shemitah—Future Tense

If the Shemitah is to manifest in the form of judgment concerning America and the American-led world order, and the American age, we can expect several things concerning its manifestation:

- The judgment will affirm the sovereignty of God over all things.

- The judgment will strike the realm of America's blessings, prosperity, and sustenance, and that of nations.

- The judgment will involve collapse.

- The judgment will humble America's pride and that of man.

- The judgment will lay bare the dependence of America and man on God.

- The judgment will separate wealth from the wealthy and possessions from the owner.

- The judgment will wipe away that which has been built up.

- The judgment will level imbalances and erase accounts within the nation and among the nations.

- The judgment will cause a cessation of functioning and an ending within America and the world.

- The judgment will bear witness against materialism within American civilization and throughout the world.

- The judgment will make clear the link between America's physical and material realm and that of the spiritual.

- The judgment will release entanglements, attachments, and bondages within the nation and among the nations.

- The judgment will strike America's economic and financial realms, and that of the nations.

- The judgment will impact the realms of labor, production, employment, consumption, revenue, and trade.

- The judgment will cause production, commerce, trade, labor, investment, profit, and trade to cease or severely decrease.

- The judgment will annul, transform, and wipe clean the financial accounts of America and the nations.

- The judgment will cause credit to go unpaid and debt to be released within America and the world.

- The judgment will wipe away that which has accumulated in America's financial realm and that of the world.

- The judgment will manifest as a sign against a nation that has driven God out of its life, rejected His ways, and pursued material blessings and idols in His place.

- The judgment will cast down the objects of America's pride and glory.

- The judgment will touch not only the financial and economic realms but every realm of society and life.

- The judgment will wipe away structure of culture, of systems, of civilization.

- The judgment will wipe away physical realities.

- The judgment will alter the landscape of nations and powers.

- The judgment will involve and affect the rise and fall of great powers.

- The judgment will call America back to God.

The Shemitah of the American Age

The issue of what lies ahead would not be complete without dealing with the prophetic warning lying at the center of the mystery. We have watched as stock markets crash, economies collapse, and that which has been built up is wiped away—and all these things joined to the Shemitah. Each of them have to do with the removal of blessing. Why is that?

The Shemitah is the reminder to any nation or civilization that its blessings come from God. And without God those blessings cannot endure. It is a warning to a nation founded on the purposes of God and blessed by God's hand, but now increasingly warring against the God of its blessings. The Shemitah is a warning to that nation that its blessings cannot endure.

And then there's the prophetic warning contained within the Hebrew, as *shemitah* literally means, "the letting fall," "the letting collapse." The warning is this: No nation can defy the ways and will of Him who is its source of blessings and expect those blessings to continue. Without Him as the foundation, the blessings will be removed and that which has been built up, no matter how highly built up, will collapse.

The "American age" and the "American Empire," as some have called it, have been highly built up. The warning here is this: if America continues on its present course, its place as the head of nations will fall and the American age and global order will be allowed to collapse.

A Great Shaking

As for things to watch: After the timing of the Shemitah, what may be of note is the timing of the last harbinger's completion—the tower at Ground Zero. Beyond that, it would be wise also to take note of America's crossing of key thresholds in its spiritual and moral descent.

Regardless of when it takes place, whether in the days of the Shemitah or beyond, I believe a great shaking is coming to this nation and to the world. I believe that this shaking will involve financial and economic collapse, though it will not necessarily be confined or limited to these realms. The collapse in the financial and economic realms may be marked, triggered, or accompanied by events in other realms. And whether figuratively, or more than figuratively, I believe will be, in one form or another, as a famine in the land.

Though such things take place as signs of national judgment, they happen also for the purpose of redemption and mercy, so that a nation hardened and deafened to God's voice may finally hear, awaken, turn, and return.

We began by overlooking the ruins of Jerusalem with the prophet Jeremiah in 586 BC. One can only imagine what he felt as he looked out into the devastation. Beyond his sorrow was the fact that he saw it all coming before it happened. What if we, in the present case, have been given an advance look and an advance warning? What do we do? If calamity should come, how do we prepare ourselves? Is there hope? And what is the answer?

To these last and critical questions we now turn.

Chapter 25

The LAST SHEMITAH

The Ruins, the Prophet, and the Hope

Is THERE HOPE? Can we avert judgment? And if judgment comes, is there hope in its midst? And after judgment comes, is there any hope in its wake?

For the answer we must return one last time to the burning ruins of Jerusalem in 586 BC. The prophet Jeremiah had warned his nation unceasingly that the day of its calamity was coming. Could they have averted it? They could have, had they turned back to God. A revival would have saved them. But that would have required repentance, a change of course, the turning away from their sins. But they refused to listen to the warning of the prophets. They refused to turn back. And the judgment came.

And *in the midst* of their judgment, was there any hope? The answer is, again, yes. The judgment had come in stages. During these stages Jeremiah still prophesied to the nation, still warned them, and still pleaded with them to follow God's will and avert total calamity. Again, they refused. And again, judgment fell.

And *after* the judgment fell, was there any hope then? Anyone who witnessed the burning of Jerusalem, the desolation of the land, and the forced deportation of the people into exile would have answered that the nation's hope was gone. Yet there *was* hope.

Had there been no hope, why would God have sent prophets, warnings, and prophecies concerning the future? But there was an even more ancient reason for hope—the mystery of the Shemitah. It was this mystery that specifically ordained that the land would lie desolate until the time was complete. At the set time the captivity would be over, the people would return, and the nation would be restored.

The Question of Hope

What about now? And what about America? Is there hope? If there was no hope, there would be no harbingers. What would be the purpose of giving warning if there was no hope of responding to that warning? If there is warning, then there is hope.

Is there any hope of America averting judgment? If there is repentance and revival, yes. But if the nation continues on its present course, then the answer is no. Does it look likely that America will turn back to God? At present and in the direction in which the nation is now proceeding, no.

What about when judgment falls—will there be hope in that day? For those who respond to God's voice and call, yes. For those who do not, no.

And after the falling of judgment or calamity, will there be hope? Yes, for all who turn to God.

Judgment or Revival, Shaking, and Calamity

So will there be judgment or revival? There can be both: judgment *and* revival. Revival can even come through judgment. There can be judgment upon a civilization and the salvation and revival for those within that civilization who turn to God.

If there is to come a great shaking, what is the hope? I would answer that it is just the opposite: with no shaking, there is little chance of hope. America has grown so hardened to God's will and so deafened to His voice, that only something of great magnitude has any hope of breaking through. It is written that God is not willing that any should perish but all should come to repentance (2 Pet. 3:9). The heart of God is to save, to restore, and to redeem. And thus all things, even shaking and calamity, must be seen through that truth.

The Fall of Idols

The Shemitah has a purpose. It manifests God's sovereignty and dominion over all things and exposes the illusion of man's sovereignty and dominion. It declares that all blessings come from God. It calls man away from the physical realm to the spiritual. It calls him to return to God. Thus the Shemitah is necessary. And when dealing with a culture or civilization enmeshed in materialism, prosperity, carnality, idolatry, arrogance, self-absorption, and the idea that man is sovereign to do however he pleases—the Shemitah becomes even more necessary.

In the day of the Shemitah's coming, illusions are exposed, entanglements are broken, pride is humbled, the gods are judged, and the idols are wiped away—even the illusions, entanglements, idols, and gods in the lives of His own people.

The Last Shemitah

Even when it comes in the form of judgment, the Shemitah is ultimately a manifestation of mercy in that it reminds, calls back, and warns—in view of a greater Shemitah yet to come. This greater Shemitah concerns not so much nations, but every individual, every life. It is the last Shemitah.

The last Shemitah declares that all things—our lives, our beings, our breath—come as gifts from God. Of ourselves we have nothing. All our notions of ownership are an illusion; all our pride, a deception. We are not sovereign but completely dependent. Everything we have—our possessions, our money, our riches, every moment of our lives—everything has been given to us.

Every heartbeat is borrowed. Everything in this world that draws us or repels us, entangles us or compels us, everything we seek after, dwell on, or live for, is temporary, fleeting, and passing away. Therefore the meaning of this life is not found in anything of this life, but only in Him who lies behind it. And the purpose of this life is not found in seeking anything of this life, but only in seeking Him who gave it.

The Shemitah, as we have seen, is connected to the number seven. In the Bible the number seven speaks of completion, the finishing, the end. The last Shemitah is that which comes at the completion of our time on the earth, the finishing, the ending of our lives. The Shemitah declares that a nation's blessings are gifts from God. The final Shemitah declares that everything and every moment we had on the earth was a gift from God. Everything we "owned" was only entrusted. It all belonged to Him, even our days.

The Shemitah separates possession from the possessor. The last Shemitah will separate us from all we owned on the earth. The Shemitah wipes away that which has been built up in the preceding period of time. The last Shemitah will wipe away all that has been built up in our time on the earth. The Shemitah brings cessation, so too the last Shemitah. As does the Shemitah, so the last Shemitah calls us away from the material realm to the spiritual. As does the Shemitah, so the last Shemitah sets free entanglements, attachments, and bondages.

As the Shemitah means "to let fall," so too the last Shemitah will be the letting fall of our earthly being and existence. As the Shemitah is observed by letting go of one's possessions, so too in the last Shemitah we will each let go of our earthly possessions and of this life itself. As the Shemitah means "release," so in the last Shemitah we will each be released of this life. And as the Shemitah draws one away from the physical and to God, so the last Shemitah will draw us away from the realm of the physical and to God.

The Final Question

Near the end of *The Harbinger* the prophet asks Nouriel a question: "And what will you do on the Day of Judgment?"

It is the ultimate question any of us could be asked. For the last Shemitah leads to eternity. We have seen the link between the Shemitah and judgment. So too the last Shemitah and the final judgment are joined together. When people hear the message of *The Harbinger,* they often ask, "What should I do in view of coming calamity?" The question is an important one. The Bible says, "A prudent man foresees evil and hides himself" (Prov. 27:12).

But regardless of whether we see the judgment of a nation or nations, the fact is we will all see the Day of Judgment. Scripture declares we will each stand before God on that day. And on that day the degree of our sins will not matter. Any sin, regardless of its nature and no matter its degree, will be infinitely and eternally judged. If we are not then right with God, if we are not then saved, if we have not received the salvation offered us, then there will be only one possibility—eternal separation from God—eternal judgment.

In the end it comes down to two destinies—heaven or hell. According to God's Word, what stands between the two eternities is not how religious we were, not how good or bad we were, or anything else but one thing: Were we born again? This fact could not be more clearly stated in Scripture: "Unless one is born again, he cannot see the kingdom of God" (John 3:3).

Yeshua

How can one be safe in the days of judgment? The answer is that in Hebrew, the word for "safety" is *yeshua*. This is the same root word from which we get the name Yeshua, which, translated into English, becomes "Jesus." In the days of a nation's judgment, and on the day of the final judgment, outside of Yeshua, Jesus, there is no safety or salvation. But inside of Him there is no fear. The key is to get one's life, every part of one's life, inside of Him who is salvation. As it is written:

> God so loved the world that He gave His only begotten Son, that whoever believes in Him should not perish but have everlasting life.
> —JOHN 3:16

The Bible records that the greatest love ever manifested in this world was the love of God in Messiah, dying on an execution stake in our place, for our sins, to bear our judgment, and then rising from that death to life, that we could be saved. How does one become born again? In the Bible it is also declared that anyone who truly receives Him, truly believes in Him, truly makes Him the Lord and Savior of their lives, and who truly follows Him as His disciple, that is the one who is born again—saved. It can begin with a decision, a prayer, a committing of one's heart, the answering of a call—the beginning of a new life.

That Which Falls and That Which Remains

As the Shemitah of the year 2001 approached its end, America saw the collapse of its two colossal towers. But when the towers fell, one object was left standing. It was a steel cross forged out of the calamity—in the midst of calamity, a symbol of hope; in the face of man's hatred, the love of God. That, in and of itself, was a sign.

The Shemitah declares that, in the end, all things will pass away, everything will collapse and fall—except this—God, His love, and His salvation. Everything else we sought after or dwelt upon will mean nothing. They will all pass away. But the love of God and His salvation will not fall, nor collapse, nor fail, but will remain forever. And the only thing that will then matter is whether we sought Him, found Him, and became right with Him—in that love and in that salvation.

Now and Forever

The Bible says "now" is the time of salvation. Now is the time to get one's life right with God. It cannot be put off until tomorrow. The only day we have is today, and the only moment, now. The time is late. Whatever is not right in your life, whatever is not of God or in His will, now is the time to rule it out of your life. And whatever God is calling you to do or be, now is the time to do it, to be it, and to rule it into your life.

The sound of an alarm cannot, by nature, be pleasant. It can't be. Otherwise it wouldn't serve its purpose to awaken and to warn. *The Harbinger* and *The Mystery of the Shemitah* are not only the revealing of mysteries but also the sounding of alarms. Whenever I've been tempted to rest from sounding the alarm, I'm reminded of God's word to Ezekiel: If the watchman sees the danger coming and doesn't sound the trumpet to warn the people, when the calamity comes, their blood will be upon his head. So I sound the trumpet.

The time is late. One way or another, judgment will come. Therefore now is the time to be saved. Now is the time to do whatever one must do to get right. And for those who will answer the call, now is the time to become great.

The alarms have gone off. The trumpets have sounded. The call has gone forth. One is left with a choice—to respond or not. *The Harbinger* closes with one final call—the last words of the prophet. I leave the one reading this with the same words:

> *Let those who have ears to hear it, let them hear it…and be saved.*

EPILOGUE

BLACK SUNS
AND
THE SEVENTH
SHEMITAH

ONE LAST NOTE: The BLACK SUNS (and the RED MOONS)

The Signs and the Moedeem

THE PHENOMENON OF solar eclipses has come up, thus far, twice. The space we have here will allow for a little more detail to be given. We have noted that the ancient rabbis saw solar eclipses as signs of judgment. The reference is found in the rabbinical writing Sukkah 29a:

> Our Rabbis taught, when the sun is in eclipse, it is a bad
> omen for the entire world…Our Rabbis taught, "When
> the sun is in eclipse it is a bad omen for those who wor-
> ship idols. But when there is an eclipse of the moon, it
> is a bad omen for Israel, since Israel reckons time by the
> moon and those who worship idols by the sun."[1]

Now, of course, solar and lunar eclipses are natural and regular phenomenon as determined by the relative movements of
the sun, the earth, and the moon. And the rabbinical writings
do not carry biblical authority. But there is a biblical basis for
connecting the darkening of the sun and moon, in specific circumstances, to judgment.

> Behold, the day of the LORD comes…For the stars of
> heaven and their constellations will not give their light;
> the sun will be darkened in its going forth, and the moon
> will not cause its light to shine.
> —ISAIAH 13:9–10

> For the day of the LORD is near…The sun and the moon
> will grow dark…
> —JOEL 3:14–15

> Immediately after the tribulation of those days the sun
> will be darkened, and the moon will not give its light.
> —MATTHEW 24:29

Black Suns and Red Moons

The events spoken of in these passages are not regular or natural occurrences, but apocalyptic events. Added to that, a solar
eclipse and a lunar eclipse cannot naturally take place at the
same time.

The Scriptures speak of the sun and the moon and the celestial lights functioning as "signs." The Hebrew word used in Genesis 1:14 is *otote*; it can also be translated as "evidence," "mark," and "omen." The same verse declares that they will be connected to days and years and "seasons." But the Hebrew word translated as seasons is *moedeem*. *Moedeem* literally means "an appointment," or "the appointed time" or "the appointed meeting." It is the same word used for the holy days of Israel. Add to this the Scriptures' emphasis on these celestial lights as signs of judgment and the end times, and we have to, at the very least, conclude that they may at times serve as signs of significant events.

With regard to lunar eclipses, it has been noted that a unique series of four such eclipses are to appear from the spring of 2014 to the autumn of 2015, each on a Jewish holiday. They have also been called "blood moons" because of the red color they acquire in the midst of the eclipse. The occurrence of four consecutive lunar eclipses, each on a Jewish holiday, has taken place only six times in the last two thousand years. Three of those times have been associated with pivotal events in Jewish history: the expulsion of the Jewish people from Spain, the rebirth of Israel, and the regaining of Jerusalem.

Is there any possible link between these occurrences and the Shemitah?

Aside from its first six months, this series of blood moons or lunar eclipses will all take place within the coming Shemitah or its autumn wake. One lunar eclipse will take place in the Tishri that begins the Shemitah. The next will appear in the spring marking the center of the Shemitah. And the final one will take place in the Tishri that ends the Shemitah and marks its climactic wake.

But what has often been missed is the significance of the solar eclipses in regard to their timing.

The Black Sun and the Harbinger

We have noted the link in timing between the darkening of the sun and the tower of Ground Zero. As the fourth of the nine harbingers, the tower already constitutes a sign of judgment. But, as we have seen, at the time the tower reached its full height, on the day the tower was crowned with its spire, the sun was darkened. The tower was crowned on the day of a solar eclipse.

Another attempt had been made to crown the tower two weeks earlier. But the endeavor had to be abandoned because of the heavy gusts of wind at the tower's summit that day. The date was April 29. On the anniversary of the first attempt to crown the tower, on April 29 of the following year, the sun was again darkened, another solar eclipse linked to the timing of the tower's ascent.

The Black Sun and the Shemitah

The phenomenon is not only connected to the tower, but, on certain occasions, to the Shemitah. The darkening of the sun has, at times, converged with the Shemitah's climactic end. This does not mean that an event of significance must occur at such a time. The convergence happened in 1959 with no apparent corresponding event of significance.

On the other hand, when the sun has darkened at the time of the Shemitah's climactic end, it has, more than once, signaled an event of great significance—and an event that just happens to take place in the same realm appointed by Scripture concerning the end of the Shemitah—the financial realm.

The Black Sun of 1931

In 1931 a solar eclipse took place on September 12. It happened at the end of the Year of the Shemitah. On the Hebrew calendar the eclipse took place on Tishri 1, the same day that ends the Shemitah and that begins at the moment of the Shemitah's climactic conclusion, at the sunset of Elul 29, the moment of financial nullification.

Eight days after the convergence, England abandoned the gold standard and set off market crashes and bank failures throughout the world. The darkening of the sun at the Shemitah's end ushered in the greatest monthlong stock market percentage crash in Wall Street history.

The Black Sun of 1987

In 1987 a solar eclipse took place on September 23. It happened at the end of the Year of the Shemitah. It took place on the exact day of that end, Elul 29, the climactic day of financial nullification.

Less than thirty days after that convergence came perhaps the most mysterious collapse in Wall Street history. The black sun had ushered in "Black Monday," the greatest percentage crash in Wall Street history. Again, the sun's darkening at the Shemitah's climactic end had brought the greatest of financial collapses in American history.

In terms of the proportion of the market wiped away, the convergence of the Shemitah's end with the black sun has marked both the blackest month and the blackest day in Wall Street history.

The Coming Black Sun

Most of the coming Shemitah will take place in the year 2015. During that year there will be two solar eclipses. The first will take place on March 20. On the biblical calendar, up until sunset, March 20 is Adar 29. From sunset on, it is Nisan 1. It is the precise mid-point of the Shemitah year. Thus, the darkening of the sun will mark the beginning of the sacred year, and the Shemitah's exact center point.

The second solar eclipse of 2015 will take place on September 13. September 13 is Elul 29—again, the very of day that constitutes the Shemitah's climactic end, the Day of Nullification.

As it did in September 1931, and again in September 1987, it will fall on the Shemitah's climactic end. In the past, this ushered in the worst collapses in Wall Street history. What will it bring in this time?

Again, as before, the phenomenon does not have to manifest at the next convergence. But, at the same time, and again, it is wise to take note.

ONE LAST MYSTERY:
The SEVENTH SHEMITAH

The Jubilee

O NE LAST MYSTERY—and one that reveals not only the Shemitah's prophetic nature but also its dynamic of redemption.

In the Bible every seventh day is a Sabbath day. Every seventh year is a Shemitah or Sabbath year. And every seventh

Shemitah leads into the year called "Jubilee." The Jubilee always follows the Year of the Shemitah.

> And you shall count seven sabbaths of years for yourself, seven times seven years; and the time of the seven sabbaths of years shall be to you forty-nine years. Then you shall cause the trumpet of the Jubilee to sound on the tenth day of the seventh month...
>
> —Leviticus 25:8–9

The word *jubilee* has come to mean a time of celebration or anniversary. But in Hebrew, the word is *yobel*. *Yobel* means "trumpet blast." The Jubilee was heralded with sounding of the trumpet throughout the land.

The Year of Setting Free

As the crowning of the seventh Shemitah, or the seventh cycle of seven years, the Jubilee was something of a super Shemitah. It was the Shemitah taken to a new level. In the Year of the Shemitah the land rested—so too in the Year of Jubilee:

> That fiftieth year shall be a Jubilee to you; in it you shall neither sow nor reap what grows of its own accord, nor gather the grapes of your untended vine.
>
> —Leviticus 25:11

In the Year of the Shemitah came release. But in the Year of Jubilee the release took on new meaning. It was not simply the letting go of land or debt. In the Jubilee, slaves and prisoners were set free. It was thus the year of liberty:

> And you shall consecrate the fiftieth year, and proclaim liberty throughout all the land to all its inhabitants.
>
> —Leviticus 25:10

The Year of Restoration and Coming Home

For those in debt the Shemitah brought restoration as all debts were wiped away. But in the Jubilee the restoration involved even more:

> It shall be a Jubilee for you; and each of you shall return to his possession, and each of you shall return to his family...In this Year of Jubilee, each of you shall return to his possession.
>
> —LEVITICUS 25:10, 13

If one had lost one's inheritance or the inheritance of one's family, in the Year of Jubilee it would be restored. The Jubilee was the year of restoration, the year of reconciliation, and the year of return. In the Jubilee, if others had taken possession of one's land, they had to relinquish it. The Jubilee saw individuals returning to their families, families returning to their ancestral homes and lands, possessions returning to their owners, and the dispossessed returning to their inheritances.

No one today knows for sure when the Year of Jubilee falls.

AD 70: The Loss of
Zion and Jerusalem

The year was AD 70. The war had begun four years earlier. It now reached its climactic moment. Jerusalem was under siege by the Roman army led by Titus, son of the newly crowned emperor Vespasian. Inside the city were chaos, division, and famine. Finally the Roman forces broke through the walls. The Temple was set on fire. Jerusalem fell. Countless thousands of its inhabitants were killed. Tens of thousands were enslaved.

Forty years earlier the Galilean rabbi Yeshua, later known as "Jesus," had prophesied that Jerusalem would be destroyed and the people would be taken captive into the nations. His words had come true. The Jewish people had lost their homeland and their most prized earthly possession, the holy city of Jerusalem. They would wander the world for almost two thousand years from nation to nation—oppressed, persecuted, and hunted down, as their land lay desolate, barren, and forbidding.

Strangers in the Land and Prophecies of Return

But biblical prophecy foretold that in the end times God would gather the Jewish people from the ends of the earth and bring them back to the land of Israel, their ancient homeland, and to Jerusalem, their holy city. The return of the Jewish people to the land of Israel is the central event of end-time prophecy. For much of the past two thousand years the idea of such a return seemed an impossibility.

Jewish people had been scattered to the ends of the earth, many having no intention of returning to their ancient land. And the land of Israel itself was in the hands of others. In AD 70 the land was taken by Roman armies. Centuries later it would be in Byzantine hands. The Byzantines were conquered by Arab armies who now claimed the land for Muhammad and Allah. Then came the Crusaders, and after them, more Muslim armies. In the fifteenth century the land fell to the Ottoman Turks, who ruled it into the twentieth century.

A Change of Empires

In the nineteenth century, revival swept through England. One of the fruits of that revival was a love for the Jewish people and the nation of Israel. Exemplifying that love was the prayer one

English boy had been taught by his mother to include in his devotions:

> O Lord, we would not forget Thine ancient people, Israel; hasten the day when Israel shall again be Thy people and shall be restored to Thy favor and to their land.[1]

It so happened that in the early twentieth century the British Empire was drawn into a war that would involve the Ottoman Turkish Empire, the power that, at the time, ruled over the land of Israel.

During the war the Ottoman Empire crumbled, and British forces led by General Edmund Allenby entered the Holy Land. The British would take the city of Jerusalem without a fight. Allenby was the boy who had prayed every night for God to restore the Jewish people to their ancient homeland. Now it was he who, as a British general, was the key instrument in bringing it about. For the first time in two thousand years the land was in the hands of a power sympathetic to the Jewish people.

The Restoration of the Land

One month before Allenby's victory in Jerusalem the British government issued the Balfour Declaration, which stated:

> His Majesty's government view with favour the establishment in Palestine of a national home for the Jewish people, and will use their best endeavours to facilitate the achievement of this object…[2]

The Balfour Declaration marked a turning point in the restoration of the Jewish people to the land of Israel—the first such turning point in two thousand years. For the first time since the Roman Empire drove the Jewish people into exile, a major power had opened up the land of Israel for the establishment of a Jewish homeland and the return of the Jewish people.

The Mystery of the Shemitah
and the Restoration of Zion

The Jubilee largely centers on the restoration of land to the dispossessed. There could never have been a greater or more momentous Jubilee for the Jewish people with regard to the restoration of the land than the issuing of the Balfour Declaration. Why is this significant here? What does it have to do with the mystery of the Shemitah?

The Jubilee must take place in the year following the Year of the Shemitah. It must begin in the autumn, on Yom Kippur, the Day of Atonement, following the end of the Shemitah, in the Shemitah's autumn wake. Allenby entered Jerusalem on December 11, 1917. The Balfour Declaration was issued one month earlier on November 2. Less than two months earlier, on September 16, 1917, the Year of the Shemitah had reached its conclusion. Thus the Hebrew year beginning in September 1917 and lasting until September 1918 constitutes "the year after the Shemitah."

Whether 1917 was the actual calendar year of Jubilee or not, we cannot say. But with regard to the two-thousand-year exile of the Jewish people from their land, it was certainly a prophetic Jubilee—a mega-Jubilee, a Jubilee of ages. And it happened to take place in the year following the Shemitah, as ordained in the ancient decree concerning the Jubilee.

The Jubilee is to be a year of restoration. After two thousand years, in the year 1917, the first official act of restoring the land to the Jewish people took place. In the Jubilee each one is to "return to his possession." In the same way, in 1917 the door opened for the Jewish people to return to their possession, the land of Israel.

In the year of Jubilee, if others had taken possession of one's land, they had to relinquish it. Likewise, in 1917 those who had possession of the land given to Israel had to relinquish. So it was that the Ottoman Turkish Empire gave up the land. They represented two thousand years of foreign rule over the land now coming to an end.

In the Jubilee each one is to "return to his family." So in 1917, with the opening of the land of Israel, Jewish people from all over the world came home and returned to their family.

In the Jubilee one returned to one's ancestral home and land. In 1917 the door opened the door for the Jewish people to return to their ancestral home, to the land of their forefathers, to their inheritance.

In the Year of Jubilee the captives are set free. In AD 70 the Jewish people were led captive into the nations. In 1917 the door opened for the ending of the nearly two-thousand-year exile, the ending of the captivity—for the captives to be set free—the Jubilee.

1967: The Six-Day War

In the spring of 1967 the Egyptian government, acting on false reports of an Israeli attack provided by the Soviet Union, ordered a full mobilization of the Egyptian military in preparation for war with Israel. On May 19 Egyptian President Nasser demanded that the United Nations (UN) peacekeeping forces leave Gaza and Sinai immediately. The UN complied. On May 22 Egypt blocked Israeli ships from the Straits of Tiran. This, which Israel saw as an act of war, combined with threats of war being issued by the surrounding Arab nations, prompted Israel to take a preemptive strike. On June 5 Israel launched Operation Focus, a series of surprise airstrikes on Egyptian and Arab air force bases. It was the beginning of the Six-Day War.

In Israel's war of independence Jordanian forces had seized the ancient city of Jerusalem. Now in the first days of the Six-Day War Israel appealed to Jordan to stay out of the fighting. But Jordan joined other Arab nations in attacking. On June 7 Israeli troops approached the ancient city of Jerusalem held by Jordanian troops. General Mordechai Gur announced to his commanders:

> We're sitting right now on the ridge and we're seeing the Old City. Shortly we're going to go into the Old City of Jerusalem, that all generations have dreamed about...[3]

Jerusalem Returned

The Israeli paratroopers entered the Lion's Gate and made their way through the cobblestone streets of the ancient city. They advanced toward the Temple Mount and the Western Wall. It was the first time that Jewish soldiers were seen in biblical Jerusalem since ancient times when the Romans destroyed it. They reach the Western Wall, the holiest site of Judaism. There, looking up at the massive stones above them, the soldiers stood in awe, many of them in tears. Spontaneously they began reciting the ancient Hebrew prayer of the *Shehechianu*:

> *Baruch Atah Adonai, Elohenu Melech Ha Olam She-hechianu, V'Kiemanu, V'Higianu Lazman Hazeh.*

> *(Blessed are You, Lord our God, King of the Universe, who has sustained us, who preserved our lives, and who has enabled us to reach this day.)*

They were then joined by Rabbi Shlomo Goren, who sounded the shofar at the Western Wall to proclaim its liberation. Goren spoke to the soldiers gathered at the wall:

> The vision of all generations is being realized before our eyes: The city of God, the site of the Temple, the Temple Mount and the Western Wall, the symbol of the nation's redemption, have been redeemed...[4]

The moment is epic. For the first time in two thousand years, for the first time since the calamity of AD 70, Jerusalem is in Jewish hands; the Holy City is restored to the Jewish people and the Jewish people to the Holy City. The moment is prophetic, a keystone in biblical end-time prophecy.

The Mystery of the Shemitah and the Restoration of Jerusalem

The Jubilee is largely focused on being restored to one's land and inheritance. Every year, on Passover, the Jewish people would conclude the ceremonial meal by saying, "Next year in Jerusalem." Now they were there. Apart from the restoration of the land itself, there could hardly have been a greater restoration for the Jewish nation in two thousand years of history than the restoration of Jerusalem. What does the restoration of Jerusalem have to do with the mystery of the Shemitah?

As we have seen, the Jubilee must take place in the year following the Year of the Shemitah. The Israeli soldiers entered the Lion's Gate on June 7, 1967. The year before this and the Six-Day War was the Shemitah. For the first time since the calamity of AD 70, Jerusalem was back in Jewish hands. The Shemitah began on September 27, 1965, and ended on September 14, 1966. The liberation of Jerusalem took place in the year following the Shemitah, as in the Jubilee.

As with the granting of the land of Israel for a Jewish homeland, the regaining of Jerusalem was a prophetic Jubilee, a Jubilee lifted up in prayer by Jewish people all over the earth for almost two thousand years, a mega-Jubilee. And as in 1917, again it took place in the year following the Shemitah.

The Jubilee is the year of liberation. In the same way, now, after almost two thousand years Jerusalem was liberated by her children.

The Jubilee is about redemption. In the same way, that which took place in 1967 was seen by Jewish people all over the world as a pivotal moment of national redemption.

The Jubilee is the year of restoration. So in 1967 Jerusalem was restored to the Jewish people and the Jewish people to Jerusalem. In the eyes of the Jewish people, a greater restoration could hardly have been imagined.

In the Year of Jubilee each one is to "return to his possession." Jerusalem was given to the Jewish people by God. Now they had returned to their possession.

In the Year of Jubilee those who had taken possession of one's inheritance have to relinquish it. In 1967 Jerusalem was relinquished by Jordanian troops, and the people of Israel entered the gates of the inheritance that had been promised them by God.

In the Year of Jubilee the people return to their ancestral homes. In 1967 the Jewish people returned to their ancestral home of Jerusalem. The fall of Jerusalem in AD 70 marked one of the greatest days of loss in Jewish history. Now what had been lost was restored—the Jubilee.

Finally, in the Year of Jubilee the shofar, the ram's horn, is sounded throughout the land, signifying freedom and restoration—thus the name Jubilee. In 1967 not only was Jerusalem restored to the Jewish people, but also at the moment of its restoration, the ram's horn was sounded at the Western Wall to signify freedom and restoration.

The Mystery of the Two Restorations

So here we have two of the most pivotal events in Jewish history, each a prophetic Jubilee, and each taking place in the year following the Shemitah, as does the Jubilee. Here are two of the greatest events of restoration in modern Jewish history, each representing the restoration of the Jewish people to their land, each representing a return, a relinquishing, a coming home, and the redemption of an inheritance—and both are linked to the Shemitah.

It all began in AD 70 when the Jewish people lost Jerusalem and the land of Israel. By the best reckonings, the period between the autumn of AD 68 and that of AD 69 was the Year of the Shemitah. That means that the destruction of Jerusalem and the loss of the land of Israel took place in the year following the Shemitah. So too each of these two calamitous losses would be reversed, redeemed, and restored in 1917 and 1967, and each likewise taking place in the year following the Shemitah.

The Seventh Shemitah
and the Time of Restoration

But there's more to the mystery. It is not only that both events take place in the days following the Shemitah, as did the Jubilee; it's also the timing between the two. The Jubilee cycle is one of seven periods of seven years—seven Shemitahs. The fiftieth year is counted also as the first year of the next seven-year period. Otherwise the cycles of the Shemitahs and the Jubilees would break apart. Thus the cycle of redemption is forty-nine years.

So how many years separated the two Hebrew years of restoration—the Hebrew year in which the British Empire restored the land to the Jewish people, and the Hebrew year in which Jerusalem was restored to Israel in the Six-Day War? The

Hebrew year of the first restoration was September 1917 to September 1918. The Hebrew year in which Jerusalem was restored was September 1966 to September 1967. The time separating the two restorations comes out to exactly seven periods of seven Hebrew years—forty-nine years—the same number of years appointed in the Bible in between restorations. It is the biblical number given for the restoration of one's land, one's possessions, and one's ancestral home. In other words, it is exactly that which happened to the nation of Israel in a cycle of forty-nine years.

Both 1917 and 1967 were epic years in Jewish history and end-time prophecy. Each involved the changing of sovereignty over the land. Each involved those in possession of the land being forced to relinquish it, the Ottoman Turks in 1917 and the Jordanian army in 1967. Each involved and came about through war, World War I in 1917 and the Six-Day War in 1967. Each involved fighting in the land of Israel. Each involved the restoration of an ancient people to their land and to their ancestral inheritance.

The first restoration followed the Shemitah of 1916 to 1917. Counting forward from that time, one arrives at the seventh Shemitah in 1965 to 1966. The seventh Shemitah leads into the year of the other great restoration: that of Jerusalem. If the cycle was to continue into the future, when would the next corresponding year be? The seventh Shemitah would be that of 2014 to 2015. Thus the corresponding year would be that of September 2015 to September 2016, beginning on Yom Kippur, the day that always ushers in the Jubilee.

Lastly, as with the other mysteries and cycles, the connection between the two restorations does not necessarily have to repeat at the end of the coming cycle—but it is worthy of note.

A PROPHETIC UPDATE FROM JONATHAN CAHN

I'VE BEEN ASKED to add an update, an additional chapter, to this special edition of *The Mystery of the Shemitah*. I'm writing this in the Shemitah's last quarter, the summer of 2015. I will share several developments—events, discoveries, and confirmations—that have taken place since the original book came out. In other words, what has happened over the course of this present Shemitah.

Witnesses on Wall Street

The Mystery of the Shemitah was released at the beginning of September 2014, just a few weeks before the Shemitah itself began. Soon after its release the discoveries or revelations contained in the book began appearing in financial newsletters, websites, blogs, even commercials. Soon after that people in the financial world began contacting me. Several contacted me to confirm the reality of the seven-year cycles. A handful of financial analysts had drawn up graphs charting those cycles. Remarkably their graphs not only charted the seven-year cycles, but also the cycles they charted converged specifically on the biblical year of the Shemitah. It was all the more striking since none of them had ever heard the word *shemitah*. And certainly none of them were trying to confirm an ancient biblical ordinance or principle.

The Bond Market Connection

Another revelation centered on the bond market. In the chapter entitled "The Cycles of Sinai" I spoke of the five major long-term collapses in the financial world in the last forty years, that of 1973, 1980, 1987, 2000, and 2007. People have asked about the Shemitah of 1994. In the book's first edition I noted 1994 mostly as an exception, but also as a demarcation of a new cycle, one of the greatest expansions in stock market history, beginning right after the Shemitah's end.

But there was something more to the story. And that something wasn't noted in the book's first printing edition since I was focusing on the rise and fall of the stock market. But there's another market—the bond market. The bond market is much larger than the stock market, about two times its volume. The Shemitah of 1994 saw a collapse of another kind. It was the year of what has been called "The Great Bond Market Massacre," considered to be the greatest collapse of the bond market up to that time. Thus, what was originally seen more as an exception turned out to be one of the greatest collapses in the financial world.[*] The Shemitah had again ushered in a collapsing of the financial realm.

Further, the bond market suffered a major collapse seven years earlier in 1987—the year of the Shemitah. That particular Shemitah saw the collapse of both the bond market and the stock market together.

1966 and the Seven Collapses

As I've sought to stress, the dynamic of the Shemitah can manifest in different ways in different cycles. It can manifest

---

[*] The one substantial update made since the first edition has been that of the Great Bond Market Massacre in the Shemitah of 1994 in the chapter "The Cycles of Sinai."

more strongly in one and not as strongly in another...nor does it have to manifest at all or become apparent in *every* cycle. And yet in the last forty years there has been a collapse in the financial or economic world at the time of the Shemitah in *every cycle.* All six cycles have seen a collapse of one form or another.

Though I chose to look at the Shemitahs of the last forty years, starting with that of 1973, what would happen if we went back further still, to the previous Shemitah? We would find yet another collapse. It's been called "The Forgotten Crash of 1966" or "The Forgettable Crash of 1966." And it likewise began in the biblical Shemitah. It was most noteworthy in that it came after a long period of economic and financial expansion. It began in the spring of 1966, just at the Shemitah's center point. It went on for eight months, going into autumn, ending just beyond the Shemitah's end. By the time it was finished, it had wiped out 22 percent of the market.[1] The Forgotten Crash of 1966 has been viewed as a harbinger of the economic and financial troubles that lay ahead and marked the beginning of a fifteen-year period of market stagnation.

Putting it together—it forms this picture: In the last *fifty years* there has been a collapse in *every single one of the Shemitah's cycles—seven collapses in all.*

The Debt Connection

The Shemitah has been linked to debt from the day it was first given at Mount Sinai. Thus, could there be a connection between the Shemitah in its modern manifestations to debt?

The strongest manifestations of the Shemitah in modern times center on two periods. The first is that of the 1930s, the Great Depression in the early part of the decade and the recession of 1937–1938 in the latter part. The other period is much longer, from the 1970s up to the present.

When, in modern times, has America's level of debt, its total debt-to-GDP ratio, reached its highest levels? The first was in the 1930s, in the midst of the Great Depression. By 1933 the debt-to-GDP ratio had reached 299 percent.[2]

The second period began in the 1970s. Since then the debt level has increased every decade, surpassing the debt levels of the Great Depression, and reaching 334 percent by 2015.[3]

Thus the two phenomena have taken place simultaneously. The dynamics of the Shemitah have manifested most strongly at precisely those times when the nation's debt has reached its highest levels. The connection that began in ancient times has held together into the twenty-first century.

The Elul 29 Simulation

Recently I came into contact with a team of financial advisors who had performed an experiment by using a computer program to simulate the algorithms of financial investments over a set period of time beginning in the early 1950s and extending to the present time, approximately sixty years. Then a second simulation was performed—the same investment was made and all the parameters were the same except one: the money was withdrawn from the stock market every seventh year, not just any seventh year, but specifically in the years beginning with the once-in-seven-year nullification point of the biblical Shemitah, Elul 29. At the end of the period the investment was returned to the market. There were no decisions or calculations made concerning market conditions, and no other strategies—just the removal of the investment once every seven years according to the time appointed in the Bible for financial nullification and its return one year later.

What was the outcome of the simulation? The results were dramatic. At the end of the period the investment that had been removed from the market at the Elul 29 of the Shemitah ended up *larger* than that which had remained in. How much larger? *Nearly 200 percent larger!*

The Early Shakings

On the very first day of the Shemitah of 2007 one of the largest banks in Britain, Northern Rock, collapsed.[4] It was the first such collapse in over a century. It would prove to be a foreshadow of what would take place on a larger scale throughout the world on the Shemitah's last day. Thus the question: Did anything of similar significance take place in the first days of the Shemitah of 2014?

The Destabilization

In the autumn of 2014 a sudden change overtook the stock market. It began to reel violently. It continued to swing wildly back and forth for several weeks. When did this change take place? It began the last week of September. It was a significant week. It was the week that began the Shemitah. The greatest crash of that opening week happened on September 25—the very day on which the Shemitah began.

The Shadow of Pestilence

One of the biblical signs of national judgment, beginning in the days of the Exodus, is that of pestilence or plague.

In the autumn of 2014 a scare overtook America. It concerned the Ebola virus, and the fear of a global epidemic. What alarmed the nation was the first appearance of the disease on American soil at the end of September. The first symptoms of the disease manifested on September 25—the opening day of the Shemitah.[5]

The Shaking

Another biblical sign of national judgment is that of literal physical shakings, calamities of nature. In the autumn of 2014 an earthquake struck American soil. Its magnitude registered 6.2 on the Richter scale. The earthquake struck on September 25—the opening day of the Shemitah.[6]

The Nuclear Dethroning

As we have seen, the word *shemitah* can be translated not only as "the release," but also as "the fall." As we have also seen, it marks the fall of powers, nations, and empires. Since *The Harbinger* I have warned that if America does not return to God, its crown as head of nations will be removed; the American age will come to an end.

One of the powers that comprise America's global preeminence is that of its military, and specifically that of its nuclear arms and capabilities.

As the Shemitah began, in its very first week, the news came out that America was dethroned. Though the margin was minimal and could be considered almost symbolic, the fact remained that America was no longer the world's strongest nuclear power. Its nuclear stock piles were now second to another power. The crown had now passed to Russia.[7]

The Economic Dethroning

In the chapter entitled "The Mystery of the Towers" I wrote of the beginning of the American age when America surpassed the British Empire in economic power. America's power on the world stage would continue to increase, becoming, in time, the world's financial center, the world's greatest creditor nation, the world's strongest military power, and the world's preeminent superpower. But it began in 1871 as America emerged as the strongest economic power on earth. I have long warned of the ending of the American age.

In the Shemitah's second week came news of a second and even more dramatic dethronement. The age that began with America's emergence as the strongest economic power on earth had come to an end. The crown had passed to China.[8] *The age that had lasted over one hundred forty years was over.* If nothing other than this had taken place in the year of the Shemitah, this event, in and of itself, would constitute a colossal shifting of geopolitical power, a seismically profound change, the ending of an old age, and the beginning of a new one.

The Persian Warning

The Book of Genesis records the beginning of an ancient law and dynamic of world history given in the city of Ur of the Chaldeans to a man named Abram:

> I will make of you a great nation; I will bless you and make your name great; and you shall be a blessing. I will bless those who bless you, and I will curse him who curses you; and in you all the families of the earth shall be blessed.
> —GENESIS 12:2–3

In other words, those people, nations, and powers that bless Israel, the Jewish people, will be blessed. Those that curse them will be cursed. Or, in other words, what you do to Israel, will be done to you.

In modern history the nation that has most blessed Israel is the United States. It is no accident that the United States has become the most blessed nation in modern times, in power, in prosperity, in security. It could be argued that this relationship was the saving grace in America's apostasy from God, a counterforce forestalling the nation's judgment.

But in recent years the relationship between America and Israel has undergone a change—descending to the lowest and most strained levels since the birth of the Jewish state. And in the year of the Shemitah the relationship has descended to still greater depths.

Twenty-five hundred years ago the Jewish people stood in danger of annihilation. The danger came from a plot devised within the government of the Persian Empire. Esther, the most prominent member of the Jewish community, decides to approach the king and warn him of the danger and plead for his intervention. The approach is against Persian protocol and can result in death. Nevertheless, Esther approaches the king. The day she approached the king is commemorated on the Jewish holy day known as the "Fast of Esther."

In the spring of 2015 the nation of Israel again stood in danger of annihilation. The danger came from the government of Iran, which had threatened Israel's destruction and was pursuing nuclear power. Iran is the modern name of Persia.

As Esther had decided to approach the throne, warn of the danger, and appeal for help, Benjamin Netanyahu, the most prominent leader in Israel, decided to approach a modern throne, the United States Congress, and there make known the danger posed by Iran and to plead for a change of course in American foreign policy. As with Esther, the approach was against protocol. Nevertheless Netanyahu made the approach. At sunset of that day it was Adar 13 on the biblical calendar— Adar 13 is the Fast of Esther, the day that commemorates

Esther's approach to the throne, to warn of the danger of annihilation over the Jewish people.

The result was that relations between the White House
and Israel reached an all-time low. Soon after Netanyahu won
reelection, the White House attacked the Israeli prime minister
along with Israel itself through public statements and the media.
The White House began increasingly bringing up the prospect
of a "reassessment" in America's relationship with Israel. It also
raised the possibility of abandoning Israel in the United Nations.

If America has been blessed in its blessing of Israel, and if this
blessing has been a saving grace and counterforce against the
nation's deepening departure from God, forestalling judgment—
then what does it mean if this saving grace and counterforce
is removed from the equation? The fact that this development
is taking place at the same moment America is descending to
unprecedented depths of moral and spiritual apostasy is ominous.

And if America abandons Israel, withdraws its support and
protection, or places Israel in danger, then what will happen
to America?

The Tectonic Moment

As I mentioned earlier in this book, in the Shemitah of 1973
a fall took place in America of a moral and spiritual nature.
The United States Supreme Court legalized the killing of the
unborn. It is significant to remind you of this because in the
present Shemitah another transformation has taken place in
America that is no less profound. When this Shemitah began,
only a small minority of states had struck down the biblical
and historic definition of marriage. But in the Shemitah's first
weeks the United States Supreme Court made the decision
not to defend the traditional definition of marriage in the
case of several state bans against changing that definition.[9]

As a result of that decision the moral landscape of America was transformed. As the Shemitah has progressed, the states that had struck down the biblical definition of marriage went from a small minority to the majority with only thirteen left that had not.

In April I was asked to speak on Capitol Hill to a gathering of leaders and members of Congress. I arrived in Washington on April 28—the day the Supreme Court heard the case concerning the future of marriage. In the late afternoon I made my way to the Supreme Court where a few believers remained standing after a day of demonstrations. One was dressed in sackcloth. Another stood by a sign that declared if the court should strike down the historic definition of marriage, it would constitute a momentous crossing of a line against God and His ways. When I spoke on Capitol Hill, I was led to warn of the consequences of crossing that line:

> Supreme Court Justices, can you judge the ways of God? Can you, with man-made verdicts, overrule the eternal laws of God? There is another court, and there is another judge. And before Him all men and all judges will give account. If a nation's high court should pass judgment on the Almighty, should you then be surprised if the Almighty should pass judgment on that court and that nation?[10]

I'm writing this update at the end of June when, just three days ago, the very line I spoke about was crossed. The Supreme Court issued its judgment. America's highest court struck down the historical and biblical definition of marriage, the covenant of man and woman. The significance of this act cannot be overstated. The definition goes back to the beginning of recorded history. The definition has not only been the foundation of human civilization but also is given in Scripture as a sacred ordinance of God.

The day after I spoke on Capitol Hill, I gave an address in Federal Hall. Federal Hall is the place where America, as a constituted nation, began, the place where its first president was sworn into office and where he issued a prophetic warning to the new nation:

> ...the propitious smiles of Heaven can never be expected on a nation that disregards the eternal rules of order and right which Heaven itself has ordained.[11]

The warning was this: If America ever turns away from God and His ways, the blessings of God would be removed from the land. If anything constitutes a nation's disregarding of "the eternal rules of order and right which Heaven itself has ordained" it must be this. The decision was tectonic. It is a sealing mark on America's apostasy from God and His ways.

If a civilization should sanctify sin, it will also profane that which is holy and call what is good "evil." The issue isn't the ultimate issue. It is only a symptom of a civilization in deep descent and apostasy from God. And the ruling not only concerned marriage, but also the Word of God, the ways of God, and the people of God. For those who hold faithful to the Word of God, except for divine intervention, the federal legalization and institutionalization of same-sex marriage will lead to a federal and institutionalized marginalization, disestablishment, vilification, and persecution. And so the words of the prophets cry out to us in warning, "Woe to those...who exchange darkness for light, and light for darkness" (Isa. 5:20, MEV).

Beyond that all these things point in one direction—judgment. In many ways the ruling was the culmination of a civilization's long fall from God. It was also the culmination of what began at the opening of the Shemitah, when the Supreme Court decided against defending marriage, a decision that witnessed a massive and rapid striking down of the biblical definition of marriage across the land—one of the most rapid moral transformations in human history.

We must keep in mind one of the most profound definitions of the Hebrew word *shemitah*—"the fall." The dramatic fall of America's moral and spiritual realms will not be limited to those realms but will be accompanied by the collapse of other realms. And if America falls, the repercussions will, of course, touch the globe and profoundly affect the course of every nation.

Convergence

What is particularly ominous is not merely the reality of all the above developments but their convergence. America's apostasy from God, and much of that of Western civilization, continues with ever increasing speed and intensity. At the same time America's relationship with Israel has deteriorated to historic depths. At the same time the harbingers have not stopped manifesting but have continued up to the present time.

The last of the nine harbingers is the tower at Ground Zero. As with the World Trade Center, the tower that has risen in its place was conceived in the year of the Shemitah. And as the Shemitah opened in the autumn of 2014, the tower too was opened, in the very first week of the Shemitah year. It is in many ways the epitome of all nine harbingers, and the most concrete and colossal monument to America's defiance. At the same time we are in the season of the Shemitah—a Shemitah that has seen the end of America's place as the number one nuclear power and economic power on earth. And as the Shemitah holds an ancient connection to debt, America's debt levels, and those of the world, now hover at astronomical levels. Add to all this the latest judgment of the Supreme Court, and we end up with a most ominous picture.

The Future and the Ultimate Issues

I have given two cautions from the beginning. The first is that we can't be dogmatic as to what *must* or must not take place in any of the Shemitah's cycles. As stated above, the dynamic can manifest itself more strongly in one cycle and more weakly in another, or not at all. That applies to the present one. What I have opened is a revelation concerning a phenomenon, a dynamic, and a pattern. But we can't be dogmatic. Nothing *has to happen* between now and the Shemitah's end or on any particular day. We are not to put our faith or focus on dates, but on God. The issue above all is repentance, not dates. It's about getting right with God. I have sought to keep all that call as the focal point. The Lord is sovereign. We cannot put God in a box. At the same time, there is another side...

My second caution is a strong as the first: *It is wise to be aware of the Shemitah's timing.* It is for that reason that I included dates in the book—not as what *must* be, but what *could* be. The phenomenon *could* manifest in the given parameters. It is for that reason that I included dates in the book. But it's not about dates. It's about getting right with God. That remains the focus and the point.

Having said all that, regardless of the timing, I believe a great shaking is coming to America and the world, a shaking that will involve a financial and economic collapse, and yet a shaking not limited to those realms. Whether the shaking or shakings take place within the parameters of the Shemitah or beyond them, whatever the timing, I believe it is wise to be ready—physically, emotionally, morally, and most of all spiritually.

It is for that reason I have written this book, to call to God those who are not in God, to call to repentance those who are not in His will, and to call His people to awaken.

—Jonathan Cahn
June 29, 2015

For MORE INFORMATION...

To FIND OUT more on what you've read in *The Mystery of the Shemitah*; to get deeper into the mysteries; to learn how to prepare for the future; to receive other related messages, insights, and prophetic updates from Jonathan Cahn; or for more about salvation or how to have a part in God's end-time work and purposes, write to:

Hope of the World
Box 1111
Lodi, NJ 07644
USA

You can also go to his website, receive free gifts, and more at HopeOfTheWorld.org, see other resources at jonathancahn .com, or get in touch by using contact@hopeoftheworld.org.

Jonathan is the leader of the Jerusalem Center/Beth Israel, a worship center made up of Jews and Gentiles, people of all backgrounds, located in Wayne, New Jersey, just outside New York City.

NOTES

Chapter 3
The Mystery of the Nine Harbingers

1. Isaiah 9:10, my translation. Since the original Hebrew of Isaiah 9:10 contains greater meaning than any single translation can render, throughout *The Harbinger* the words of this particular verse were translated and expounded upon directly from the original Hebrew. The New King James Version, renders Isaiah 9:10 in this way: "The bricks have fallen down, / But we will rebuild with hewn stones; / The sycamores are cut down, / But we will replace them with cedars."

2. Washington File, "Text: Senator Majority Leader Daschle Expresses Sorrow, Resolve," September 13, 2001, http://wfile.ait.org .tw/wf-archive/2001/010913/epf407.htm (accessed July 1, 2014).

Chapter 7
Fourth Key: The Secret Israel

1. GreatSeal.com, "First Great Seal Committee—July/August 1776," http://www.greatseal.com/committees/firstcomm/ (accessed July 2, 2014).

2. Gabriel Sivan, *The Bible and Civilization* (New York: Quadrangle/New York Times Book Company, 1974), 236. Viewed online at Google Books.

3. See, for example, John Winthrop, "A Model of Christian Charity," http://religiousfreedom.lib.virginia.edu/sacred/charity .html (accessed July 7, 2014).

Chapter 9
The Fingerprints of the Mystery

1. Jonathan Cahn, *The Harbinger* (Lake Mary, FL: FrontLine, 2011), 163.

Chapter 11
The Cycles of Sinai

1. Al Ehrbar, "The Great Bond Massacre," *Fortune*, February 3, 2013, http://fortune.com/2013/02/03/the-great-bond-massacre -fortune-1994/ (accessed June 16, 2015).

2. Alen Mattich, "Investors Should Remember 1994," Wall Street Journal, December 29, 2010, http://blogs.wsj.com/source/2010/12/29/remembering-1994/ (accessed June 16, 2015).

3. Ehrbar, "The Great Bond Massacre."

Chapter 14
The Shemitah and the Great Recession

1. Cahn, *The Harbinger*, 136.

Chapter 17
The Four Towers

1. Cahn, *The Harbinger*, 199–201.

Chapter 21
The Reigning

1. Gideon Rachman, "The Bretton Woods Sequel Will Flop," *Financial Times*, November 10, 2008, http://www.ft.com/cms/s/0/0b3da1e6-af4b-11dd-a4bf-000077b07658.html#axzz36POxAKZz (accessed July 3, 2014).

Chapter 23
The Last Tower

1. Mary Bruce, "'One Today': Full Text of Richard Blanco Inaugural Poem," ABC News, January 21, 2013, http://abcnews.go.com/Politics/today-richard-blanco-poem-read-barack-obama-inauguration/story?id=18274653 (accessed July 3, 2014).

2. Ibid.

Epilogue, Part 1
One Last Note: The Black Suns (and the Red Moons)

1. See Judeo-Christian Research, "The Babylonian Talmud, Sukkah," http://juchre.org/talmud/sukkah/sukkah2.htm (accessed July 15, 2014).

Epilogue, Part 2
One Last Mystery: The Seventh Shemitah

1. Edmund Allenby, as quoted in *God's Little Devotional Book for Students* (N.p.: Honor Books, 2003), 281. Viewed online at Google Books.

2. The Avalon Project, "Balfour Declaration 1917," Lillian Goldman Law Library, Yale Law School, http://avalon.law.yale.edu/20th_century/balfour.asp (accessed July 3, 2014).

3. Jewish Virtual Library, "The Six-Day War: The Liberation of the Temple Mount and Western Wall," http://www.jewishvirtual library.org/jsource/History/1967lib.html (accessed July 3, 2014).

4. SixDayWar.org, "1967: Reunification of Jerusalem," http://www.sixdaywar.org/content/ReunificationJerusalem.asp (accessed July 3, 2014).

A Prophetic Update
From Jonathan Cahn

1. Larry M. Elkin, "The Forgettable Crash of 1966," Palisades Hudson Financial Group, January 28, 2014, http://www.palisades hudson.com/2014/01/the-forgettable-crash-of-1966/ (accessed June 16, 2015).

2. Robert Lenzner, "QE2 Is a Goldmine for Traders, Shafts the Rest of U.S.," Forbes.com, http://www.forbes.com/2010/11/13/bernanke-obama-gold-commodities-markets-silver-inflation-deflation.html (accessed June 16, 2015).

3. Macrotrends.net, "Debt to GDP Ratio Historical Chart," http://www.macrotrends.net/1381/debt-to-gdp-ratio-historical-chart (accessed June 16, 2015).

4. BBC News, "Timeline: Northern Rock Bank Crisis," http://news.bbc.co.uk/2/hi/business/7007076.stm (accessed June 16, 2015).

5. Michelle S. Chevalier et al., "Ebola Virus Disease Cluster in the United States—Dallas County, Texas, 2014," http://www.cdc.gov/mmwr/preview/mmwrhtml/mm63e1114a5.htm (accessed June 16, 2015).

6. Armand Vervaeck, "Earthquakes in the World on September 25, 2014 (M4.5 or more)....," Earthquake-Report.com, September 25, 2014, http://earthquake-report.com/2014/09/25/earthquakes-in-the-world-on-september-25-2014-m4-5-or-more/ (accessed June 16, 2015).

7. Matthew Bodner, "Russia Overtakes U.S. in Nuclear Warhead Deployment," *Moscow Times*, October 3, 2014, http://www.the moscowtimes.com/business/article/russia-overtakes-us-in-nuclear-warhead-deployment/508409.html (accessed June 16, 2015).

8. RT.com, "China Surpasses US as World's Largest Economy Based on Key Measure," October 10, 2014, http://rt.com/business/194264-china-surpass-us-gdp/ (accessed June 16, 2015).

9. David Masci, "What Today's Supreme Court Decision Means for Gay Marriage," Pew Research Center, October 6, 2014, http://www.pewresearch.org/fact-tank/2014/10/06/what-todays-supreme-court-decision-means-for-gay-marriage/ (accessed June 16, 2015).

10. From the author's personal speech that he gave on Capitol Hill.

11. "Washington's Inaugural Address of 1789," National Archives and Records Administration, http://www.archives.gov/exhibits/american_originals/inaugtxt.html (accessed July 2, 2015).

ABOUT the AUTHOR

JONATHAN CAHN CAUSED a stir throughout America and around the world with the publication of his first book, *The Harbinger*, which became an immediate *New York Times* best seller. The book brought him to national and international prominence and countless appearances on television and in the media. Long before the book, he was known for opening up the deep mysteries of Scripture and for teachings of prophetic import. He leads Hope of the World ministries, an international outreach of teaching, evangelism, and compassion projects for the needy. He also leads the Jerusalem Center/Beth Israel, a worship center made up of Jews and Gentiles, people of all backgrounds, just outside New York City, in Wayne, New Jersey. He is a much sought-after speaker and appears throughout America and the world. He is a Messianic believer, a Jewish follower of Jesus. For more information, to find out about over two thousand other messages and mysteries Jonathan has given, for free gifts, to be part of, or to contact his ministry, write to:

Hope of the World
Box 1111
Lodi, NJ 07644
USA

Or visit his website at
HopeOfTheWorld.org

You can also visit his Facebook site (Jonathan Cahn) or a resource site at jonathancahn.com, or send an e-mail to contact@hopeoftheworld.org.

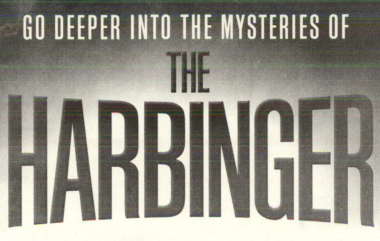

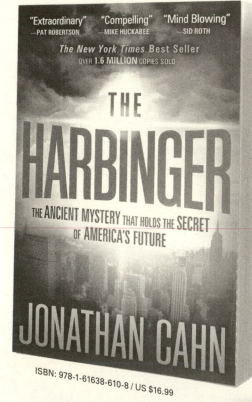

If you've been touched by this book and want to see as many people as possible receive its powerful message, we invite you to join the movement of people spreading the word about...

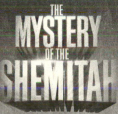

Many people who have read *The Mystery of the Shemitah* are convinced this book is a must-read for every American. Not only is this a compelling and shocking wake-up call for our nation. It offers one of the most unique revelations of God's love and desire to see His people return to Him that has ever been written. This book will not only inspire people who already know Him with new insight into His nature but also intrigue and engage people who are not yet aware of His involvement in their lives.

The Mystery of the Shemitah's timely prophetic message for our country has resonated with many internationally known ministry leaders who have gotten behind the promotion of its message. As a result, within days of its release, it made the *New York Times* best seller list and is expected to remain in high demand for a long time to come. As great as this type of promotion is, word of mouth is still the most effective way for a book to gain traction in the wider culture. If you have been moved by the message of this book, you may already be thinking of ways to let others know about it. Here are some suggestions:

- Check with your book dealer (both local and online) to see if special deals are available for bulk purchases.

- Give the book as a gift to family, friends, and even strangers. They get not only an intriguing page-turner but also insights into the nature of God that are seldom presented in our culture.

- Like the book on Facebook (www.facebook.com/theofficialharbinger). Talk about the book on social media sites, websites, blogs, and other places you engage with people on the Internet. Instead of making it an advertisement, share how the book has impacted your life. Recommend that others read it as well and link them to www.shemitahbook.com.

- Write a book review for your local paper or favorite magazine (in print or online).

- Ask your favorite radio show or podcast to have the author on as a guest.

- If you own a business, consider putting a display of these books on your counter for employees or customers.

- If you know people (authors, speakers, etc.) with a platform that enables them to speak to a wide audience, ask them to review a copy and make some comments on their websites, in newsletters, etc.

- Buy multiple copies as gifts for shelters, prisons, and rehabilitation centers where people can be provoked and encouraged by the book's timely message.

- If you're a leader, minister, speaker, communicator, or in media, let your people, your audience, or your congregation know to get it and to give it out to all who need to hear the message.

www.ShemitahBook.com